Never Trust a Thin Cook
and Other Lessons from Italy's
Culinary Capital

Other Books by Eric Dregni Published by the
University of Minnesota Press

In Cod We Trust: Living the Norwegian Dream

*Midwest Marvels: Roadside Attractions across Iowa, Minnesota,
the Dakotas, and Wisconsin*

Minnesota Marvels: Roadside Attractions in the Land of Lakes

Never Trust a Thin Cook and Other Lessons from Italy's Culinary Capital

Eric Dregni

University of Minnesota Press

Minneapolis

London

Earlier versions of these essays were published in the *Star Tribune, Modena e Modena, ICI Campus Gazette Milano,* and *Tutto Vacanze,* as well as in the book *Grazie a Dio non sono bolognese! Un americano a Modena,* published in Italian by Il Fiorino in 2003.

Published by the University of Minnesota Press
111 Third Avenue South, Suite 290
Minneapolis, MN 55401-2520
http://www.upress.umn.edu

Library of Congress Cataloging-in-Publication Data

Dregni, Eric, 1968-
  Never trust a thin cook and other lessons from Italy's culinary capital / Eric Dregni.
    p. cm.
  ISBN 978-0-8166-6745-1 (hardcover : alk. paper) — ISBN 978-0-8166-6746-8
(pbk. : alk. paper)
  1. Food habits—Italy—Modena. 2. Cookery, Italian. 3. Cookery—Italy—Modena.
4. Restaurants—Italy—Modena. 5. Dregni, Eric, 1968- 6. Americans—Italy—Modena—
Biography. 7. Food writers—Italy—Modena—Biography. 8. Modena (Italy)—Social life
and customs. 9. Modena (Italy)—Description and travel. 10. Modena (Italy)—Biography.
I. Title.
  GT2853.I8D74 2009
  394.1'20945421—dc22

                                                        2009017800

Printed in the United States of America on acid-free paper

The University of Minnesota is an equal-opportunity educator and employer.

20 19 18 17 16 15 14 13 12 11 10 09   10 9 8 7 6 5 4 3 2 1

For Piccola Katy,
the siren at the Leaning Tower of Pizza,
who took a ride on my Lambretta
and dropped everything to go on this adventure.

TORINO ASTI MILANO BRESCIA
LAMBRETTA POLENTA PORCINI
TRENTO VERONA CORTINA
PROSECCO GALILEO! PALMANOVA
GENOVA SAN REMO
PARMA PROSCIUTTO REGGIO MARANELLO
MODENA ACETO BOLOGNA PADOVA
VENEZIA TRIESTE RAVENNA
PISA LEGHORN PONTEDERA FIRENZE
IMOLA RIMINI
ELBA SIENA SAN MARINO URBINO ANCONA
ASSISI PESCARA
COSTA SMERALDA
SARDEGNA
CAGLIARI
VATICANO ROMA
GELATO
CAFFE NAPOLI LA PIZZA FOGGIA
ISCHIA CAPRI VESUVIO
AMALFI BUFALA CALCIO CAMPIONI DEL MONDO!
PAESTUM BARI
TRULLI
BRINDISI
ITALY
CALABRIA
MARSALA PALERMO STROMBOLI
SICILIA ETNA CATANIA
AGRIGENTO

Contents

Preface

I simply want to live in the place with the best food in the world. My scope has been narrowed to Italy: the country of beautiful chaos, the land of the *dolce vita*. But where in this nation of nearly sixty million people can I find the ideal meal? I learned the language by living in Lombardia for almost two years, attending high school in Brescia and then staying in Milan. I ate excellent food but know I can find better. I traveled up and down *il bel paese,* or the "beautiful country," as the Italians like to call it. I could find great restaurants in Rome, Milan, Florence, or any of the big cities, but I paid dearly for it and was surrounded by throngs of tourists unwittingly including me in their snapshots. Or perhaps it was intentional and they thought I was a typical Italian glutton.

Although I love the hustle and bustle of Milan, I am shocked to find it is one of the few places in Italy where the nine-to-five workday does not allow for the essential three-hour lunch break at home to enjoy excellent food: *risotto alla milanese, osso buco* . . . Bars in the center of the city serve meals that people gulp *in piedi come un cavallo,* or standing like a horse. On the weekend, the Milanesi rush out of town to the countryside for the tastiest Italian dishes. Why not just live at the source? What's the point of living in Italy if I'm not eating fantastic food at every meal?

I have searched for years and eaten many mediocre meals to reach this conclusion. I have written about eating beef brains in Brescia and garlic ice cream in Lecco. I have learned that basil and oregano are enemies, that arugula is socialist, and that if I dare cut my spaghetti, all the flavor goes away, or at least that's what my offended host told me as he clenched his steak knife. I know I am close to culinary nirvana when I go to Bologna—the town that many Italians consider to have the best Italian cuisine. Still, hectic modern life has enveloped Bologna as well, so I scour its region, Emilia-Romagna, for smaller cities with authentic charm unspoiled by polluted air, where people take the time to cook and enjoy their meals.

And I have found the perfect town. At last, my quest is over. Modena is plunked down on the flattest fog-covered plain of northern Italy, but, boy, can they cook! I convince my girlfriend Katy that we should quit our jobs and live abroad for two years. Katy may be hesitant to live in a country where she doesn't speak the language or know the culture, but at least we'll eat well. After all, this is the best place on earth for food.

Katy will teach Italian kids English, and I will have a part-time job writing a column for a local Modenese weekly about an American living in Italy. I'll try to infiltrate the secret balsamic vinegar societies, get behind the scenes at the Ferrari and Maserati factories in town, and be properly caffeinated with thimble-sized shots of espresso. Most of all, I hope to reveal the tricks of making tortellini, indulge in generous helpings of prosciutto and Parmigiano-Reggiano, and write about the good life in Italy with restaurant reviews of all the fanciest *trattorie*.

My friends in Milan laugh when I mention that we're moving to this small provincial city. "They're too open and friendly in Emilia-Romagna. Even their accent is open sounding!" my friend Anna says.

"So where did you meet Katy?" Giovanni asks.

I explain that we haven't been going out very long, but she is going to quit her job and move to Italy with me. We met at the Leaning Tower of Pizza.

"Pisa. It's in Pisa," Giovanni corrects me.

When I tell him that it's a pizzeria in south Minneapolis, he responds, "It's always about food with you, isn't it?"

Vicolo Forni

The little street below the new apartment Katy and I are living in is a miniature Italy. The older women in mothball-smelling minks cordially greet each other, then stop for a look into the jewelry store. The shopkeepers from the market, dressed in their white smocks, dotted with blood if they're butchers, gulp their coffee and discuss last night's soccer game in front of Maurizio's bar, Il Cappuccino. A couple of women walk by showing off the latest skintight fashion—this year everything is lavender—and act as if the men at the market aren't staring at them. Ermes leans his bicycle on the wall and shouts "Ciao bimbi" as he runs into the market to do the daily shopping for his *trattoria*. The signora from upstairs pulls at the leash of her two eager dogs, which have stopped to drool over goodies in Franco's pet store. Students with blue hair that matches their backpacks run to school munching on fresh *focaccia*. Mothers push their strollers with little *bambini* so bundled up that they can't move, and other mothers mercilessly coo over them and pinch their fat cheeks.

The gypsy woman with the screaming baby has been replaced by a bearded bum, who holds court over the alley as if everyone has come to visit him. "Buon giorno, signori," he greets with a booming monotone to every new guest to the street. He puts a whistle to his lips to get people's attention,

1

then breaks into a political speech against the mayor, interrupted only by an occasional swig from his carton of red wine and a musical interlude of *liscio* (polka) music on his tape deck.

A huge van from the market turns down Vicolo Forni and spoils the scene. The pedestrians have to line up with their backs against the wall while the big truck insists on fitting down the *vicolo*, or alley, with only millimeters to spare. Maurizio, the *barista*, has started a campaign to shut down the street to cars since it's only fifteen feet wide and eighty feet long. The bum has made the most of these interruptions to his speeches. Now he yells "Avanti!" and uses his whistle to direct traffic.

Our apartment looks over Vicolo Forni and the fantastic food market. At 5 a.m. the first vans roll in from southern Italy full of fresh mozzarella and Sicilian fruit. About 7 a.m., we enter the market for fresh rolls with raisins. The first section is the fish stand, where the smells wake us up better than double espresso. Then there's the eccentric mushroom lady, who has the best porcini in town, and the unhappy couple at the cheese stand, who are overly polite. Unless we feel like an in-depth political debate, we slip by the friendly butcher, who discusses the crazy death penalty in the United States as he chops huge cuts of beef with his cleaver.

Rosella and her husband, Luigi, at the fruit stand are the friendliest at the market. She helps us with cooking advice as well as keeps us abreast of new gossip in the market. They've been awake since four o'clock unloading and preparing their beautiful display of everything from dandelion greens to zucchini flowers. When I tell Luigi that supermarkets in the United States are often open twenty-four hours, his jaw drops, and he exclaims, "Twenty-four-hour stores? But that's perverse!"

At first, Katy is terrified of the market because the vendors are quick to yell at anyone who dares touch the merchandise. Customer service is approached very differently in Italy and quickly determines which stands are our favorites.

If you forget to take your *scontrino*, or receipt, the vendors will come screaming after you with it. All cash registers are controlled by the Guardia di Finanza, the Italian IRS, and sometimes they do random checks to nab shopkeepers doing transactions *in nero* (under the table). Both the customer and the owner could go to jail if caught, I'm told. Scandal erupts across Italy at the injustice against a grandfather who is put on trial because he gave his grandson a chocolate bar in his store without a receipt.

Perched on the corner of a building in Modena's Piazza Grande, where the market used to be, stands a little medieval statue named "La Buona" (the Good One), who watches to make sure everyone is honest. She strikes the fear of God into the hearts of shopkeepers who consider putting their thumb on the scale.

Once we learn the protocol, both Katy and I view the market as the perfect opportunity to spruce up our Italian. She looks at the shopping list and sees *orecchiette* (ear-shaped pasta). She asks at the fresh pasta stand, "Vorrei un sacco di orecchi!" (I'd like a sack of ears!). The woman responds matter-of-factly, "Oh, you'll have to go to the butcher for that." At the pork butcher next to Il Cappuccino, Katy asks for a *uomo* (man) rather than a *uovo* (egg). They point at me and ask, "What's wrong with him?"

They're always teasing each other—and us—at the pork butcher. After I ask how the four men and women who work there are related—brothers-sisters, cousins, husband-wives—

one of the guys asks me loudly, "Do you really think I'd marry her? Look how old she is!" She brushes it off, "He thinks he's so young." Then she turns to me, "How old do you think I am?" I don't dare answer, and they all break out laughing, "If you can't laugh about it, what's the point of living?"

When I romanticize about our life next to the market in the medieval center of Modena, Katy cuts me off. Especially when I say the white marble bell tower of the cathedral is our twelfth-century alarm clock, she says, "It's still an alarm clock, and who wants to be woken up?" I rave about a lunch I've made of polenta, Tuscan white beans, and wild boar sausage. She rebuts, "Oh come on, it's just cornmeal mush and beanie weenies! Stop getting all flowery; you're as bad as Franny Mayes and her villa-in-Tuscany nonsense."

The bum who diverts traffic in the alley shows up every morning at nine o'clock. This morning he's especially animated. A group of high school students are listening to him before school. Maurizio steps out of his bar and notices the bum giving lessons. "Looks like we've adopted him, no?" he tells us.

In spite of the bum's steady diet of cheap red wine, his memory is sharp. The bum greets an older man walking to the market. "Buon giorno, I see you've bought a new shopping cart."

The man turns around surprised, "Well, yes . . . I did."

"Very nice. Very nice. Maybe you could have picked out a nice bright blue rather than black, though. It would be a little more cheery and festive."

Other people in the alley turn around and notice his little shopping cart and agree with the bum. "It's true. The black is nice, but blue would have been better. Why did you get black?"

The man is almost at the other end of the alley when he finally is forced to say, "OK, OK, I should have gotten the blue shopping cart!"

The other regular in Vicolo Forni is Franco who owns the pet store. He's usually chatting outside his shop or in Maurizio's bar, and he pets all the passing dogs. He greets us with a big smile. If we pause for a minute to talk, it easily turns into half an hour. He's pleased to find out Americans are living in Vicolo Forni and recalls how he and his wife once won a trip to *La Grande Mela*, or the Big Apple. "All the skyscrapers are very beautiful," he tells us, "but I finally knew I was in America when I went inside one of the offices. There it was at the end of a corridor!" He pauses and gestures for emphasis. "A big glass water dispenser! Now this I have to try! I went up to it, put my cup under it, and the machine went 'blurble, blurble' just like in all the television programs I've seen for fifty years. Then, I knew I was in America."

By eleven o'clock, the smells from the Trattoria Aldina next door seem to seep right through the wall. At first, the odors are nice and tempt us to stop for tortellini and *zampone*, but soon we fling open the windows for some fresh air. Friday's fish fry is especially pungent. Regardless, we often break down and stop in the restaurant for some fresh pasta and *torta di spinaci* (spinach and ricotta cake).

Occasionally, we see the cook from Aldina when we're at the market buying vegetables from Rosella. She tells me, "Bravo, bravo. It's better that you don't come to eat at the trattoria all the time. Save your money like good kids."

By one o'clock, Vicolo Forni has calmed down as everyone rushes home—or to Trattoria Aldina—to have lunch. One day, I hear a big crunch downstairs on the alley as a truck driver eager to get home to his pasta misjudges the size of the alley and mashes my bicycle against the wall. By the time I get downstairs, the truck is gone, but Maurizio tells me he has compiled almost enough signatures so the alley will be closed to traffic any time. Who knows, maybe Maurizio could set up a stage for our newly adopted bum to dance to his polka music?

All the stores close until 4 p.m. for maximum digestion of the lunchtime pasta and then stay open until 7:30 p.m. At night, the area around the market is a ghost town but is only taking a break before the whole scene repeats itself the next day.

Permesso di Soggiorno

The stamps in our passports from the Malpensa airport allow us three months in Italy. Technically, if we're ever stopped by the police within the ninety days, this visa should work. In reality, they will tell us to register at the *questura*, or police station, in Modena, so they can keep tabs on all the usual suspects.

All foreigners staying for more than a week in one place are required to register for the dreaded *permesso di soggiorno*, or permission to stay. The European Union nullified this law years ago for E.U. members, but Italian bureaucracy hobbles along, and the police still claim all Europeans must have this document or face the consequences. Since we are from the United States, we get in line with everyone else.

My friend Giovanni thinks we're crazy to bother to get a *permesso di soggiorno*. I explain that getting a *permesso di lavoro*, or work visa, is nearly impossible, and we want to stay at least a year. We at least need some sort of documentation since Katy is going to teach English and I'll teach and write for a newspaper. Giovanni explains the futility of obeying the law, pointing out that hundreds of corrupt officials never went to jail or even paid a fine after the *mani pulite* (clean hands) bribery scandal. "It's best to just do what you have to do," he tells me. "If you get caught, try to get out of it. Just don't draw attention to yourself."

I ignore Giovanni's advice, and Katy and I line up outside the *questura* in Modena with dozens of other foreigners, mostly from Eastern Europe and Africa. I ask people in
line how long they've been waiting, but no one understands
English—or Italian. When the guard wielding a submachine
gun steps away for a moment, Katy and I peek inside to see
if this is even the correct line. The building has oppressively
large doors to show those who enter how insignificant they
are compared with the greatness of the Italian government.
The rubber soles of our shoes squeak loudly on the marble
floors, showing that we can't make a smooth entrance, and
the institutional dust bunnies have numerous babies blowing down the halls. We walk alongside the line of foreigners
into a muggy room with a few bureaucrats aggressively
smoking behind their glass windows under the large sign
"vietato fumare," no smoking.

The line leads to two windows: one for people from
North Africa and Eastern Europe, another for Asia. No one
stands in front of the North America window, so Katy waits
while I step up for my *permesso di soggiorno*. I knock on the
glass to get the attention of an officer blowing smoke rings,
sipping espresso, and reading the pink sports newspaper
Gazzetta dello Sport. He's annoyed and holds up a finger to
tell us to wait a minute. He casually pages through the re-
maining pages of the paper, snubs his cigarette, and asks,
"Cosa vuoi?" (What do you want?).

I politely explain that we need a *permesso di soggiorno*
and hand him our passports and the necessary documents.

"You? But you're American!"

I tell him that we need the proper identification if we're
going to stay in Modena.

"No, no, no. Don't worry," he says and moves his hands

as though he's whisking us away. "You go take your trip and have fun in Italy."

"But we want to stay in Modena for a couple of months," I say, "so we need a *permesso di soggiorno.*"

Now he's suspicious. "Why on earth would you want to stay here in Italy when we all want to go to the United States?" he asks, as though he's our Virgil warning us before we descend into inferno.

I have to convince him of our motives—without revealing that we want to work—before he'll help us out. "Well, Italy is so beautiful: the architecture, the mountains, the sea . . . "

"—and the women!" he interrupts.

"Yes, the women are beautiful," I agree, and Katy gives me a dirty look. I recover by adding, "And, of course, the food here is so good. *Si mangia proprio bene!* Pizza, pasta, tortelloni, *tartufi* . . . "

He nods, gently strokes his beard while thinking to himself. "Yes, yes, this is true, very true," he says as though lost in his imaginary dinner. Or maybe he's picturing a terrible world without Italian food and feels pity on us, "OK, I'll let you enter and help you with your documents."

A Page Boy in Pavarotti's Restaurant

Modena is home to Maserati, Ferrari, and De Tomaso cars, but far more important, to Luciano Pavarotti. The operatic tenor known throughout the world was the symbol and essence of Modena. Not for his voice, which by any measure faded as his girth grew, but for his belly, which bore testament to the fantastic food of Emilia-Romagna. Pavarotti was born and fed here on a steady diet of *prosciutto crudo*, tortellini, Parmigiano-Reggiano, and balsamic vinegar. This is why Modena is the place for me.

Unable to sleep one early morning, I wander through the Piazza Grande of Modena and discover a group of dancers dressed in beautiful Renaissance costumes swirling elegantly to waltzes. I hurry home to grab my camera and am soon taking snapshots of this colorful group amid RAI TV cameras. One of the dancers, wearing a padded crown in her hair and a black dress with gold stitching, asks me why I'm taking photos of this precursor to the annual town festival.

"I'm writing an article about Modena for my newspaper in the United States," I exaggerate. Actually, I don't know anyone at my hometown paper in Minneapolis, but I am writing a column on my experiences in Italy for the weekly newspaper of Modena, which pays me $15 a week—apparently not enough to live on.

"We are all journalists, too! My name is Marina; I must tell the others," she says and begins introducing me to the others in their elegant outfits as an important writer for American newspapers. They are dressed in the old royal garb so RAI television can film a preview for Modena's summer festival. I meet Fabio (in a bright red page-boy outfit), Luca (with a three-cornered feathered cap and the Duke of Este's robe), Stefano (in black tights and a puffy baron's gown), and Laura (with a gigantic hoop skirt and six-inch shoulder pads). I whisper to Marina that I'd like to be a bigwig journalist but have only had small articles published.

"Oh, just tell everyone you're a journalist and soon enough you will be," she replies positively. She whisks me inside the city hall building on the edge of the piazza, where the mayor and other local businessmen are receiving the dance company under sweeping frescos of battle scenes on the ceiling. Marina convinces the leader of the troupe to dress me in an extra costume—a ridiculously tight, brightly colored page-boy outfit—for entry into a fancy dinner that evening at Pavarotti's restaurant.

I feign illness to my boss and cancel all my evening classes to go see the fat man in person. Unfortunately, Luciano doesn't show up for this invitation-only party where medieval attire is required. Some guests speculate he's on tour; others guess his tax fraud problems are pestering him again. A Modenese judge had dismissed the charges, but a judge from rival Bologna wouldn't let him off the hook and reinstated the indictment. Only after we ate at his restaurant did we hear that Pavarotti was getting so big he couldn't get around without help.

Modena's mayor sits at the head of the table with other dignitaries. When I get a chance to speak with him, I suggest the city of Modena open the ancient canals in the city center that used to run all the way to Venice. The mayor smirks at me and puts his left hand on the inside of the elbow joint of his right arm. I assume he's telling me *vaffanculo*, or fuck off, but he has a disappointed frown on his face. He's gesturing that the rats that would come out of the canals are this big, from fingertips to elbow. Our strange conversation is interrupted when discotheque music by the poppy Danish band Aqua is blasted into the dining hall and a few people dressed in medieval noble outfits dance to the techno beat. Pavarotti never shows up to sing an aria to the crowd. Instead, fake dukes, barons, and earls flail their arms in glee as they dance to the rhythm of "Barbie Girl."

Sleeping with Nuns

Our apartment in Vicolo Forni used to be the chapel of a convent dating back to the fourteenth century. Latin inscription is carved into the walls, wooden beams two feet wide hold up the terra cotta ceiling tiles, and floor-to-ceiling arched windows open up to the food market and the tiny alley of Vicolo Forni below.

Katy feels at home living in a chapel after attending Catholic schools her whole life. I, on the other hand, went to Catholic school for one year, when I was four, but the nuns hit us kids, locked us in closets, and tied naughty children to trees for the others to taunt. I expect to have visions of evil nuns flying over my bed at night, but the apartment is relaxed, unlike many of the nuns I've known.

The apartment is a fortress with five locks on the only door and an iron gate for extra protection. The landlord suggests we use all the locks to keep out the legions of burglars prowling around the streets. This idea of the house as an impenetrable stronghold must stem back to medieval times. Villas in the country are surrounded by enormous gates and walls with broken glass cemented into the top, and windows on the ground floor have bars covering them.

I tell one of my Italian friends that it's rare to find iron bars over windows in the United States except in jail or, of course, New York City and Washington, D.C. He replies,

"I dream of seeing houses without gates, bars on the windows, or locks. Is it true that your grass doesn't have a fence around it and a paper boy delivers a newspaper to your door? This is very beautiful." He doesn't believe me, however, when I explain that in rural areas, people sometimes leave their keys in their car's ignition.

An Italian house's second line of defense is the heavy wood or metal shutters over the windows, which are bolted up tight each night. Even though we're on the second story, one of our Italian friends is horrified our new apartment has enormous windows without shutters. "That's probably why they couldn't rent it," he suggests. "People can see in. They can see all your things!" I argue we don't have anything to steal—just books and clothes—so it's better that they see a burglary would be futile. He doesn't agree with my reasoning.

Break-ins give newspapers constant headlines. "Polpette rubate durante furto con scasso!" (Meatballs stolen in burglary) screams the front page posted at the newsstand. I overhear a couple of old men looking at this shocking news, "Now that's going too far! Have they no decency?"

Katy and I introduce ourselves to our neighbor upstairs, who has two little watchdogs. Although they make an enormous racket by clicking their paws on the floor and barking like crazy every time the doorbell rings, the dogs have been fed so much by the old woman that they can barely waddle around. Thieves only hear the furious barking behind her fortified doors.

She warmly takes my hands and asks us where we come from. "Minnesota," Katy replies.

"Minestra! Like minestrone!" our neighbor says excitedly. "Oh, so you're a very good cook then! Brava!"

We ask if we can leave our bikes in the communal stair-well since we've heard about all the thieves in town. She tells us that unfortunately other neighbors think bicycles are an eyesore in the hall. "C'è cattiveria in questo edificio!" (There's wickedness in this building!), she says while mak-ing the *corna* gesture to ward off the evil eye. Once again, visions of evil nuns haunt me.

In spite of these warnings of meatball burglars and wicked neighbors, we keep our door only triple-locked since we don't want to spend ten minutes fastening and unfas-tening the locks each time we step out.

More pressing problems have arisen. We can't hook up the heat, water, and electricity without official residency doc-uments, and even connections at the *questura* can't help. The necessary forms take weeks to get even if we were legal and where are we supposed to live until they've been processed? In getting the necessary documents, I notice that my Min-nesota driver's license has expired. Even though at home I just need to read an eye chart of letters for the vision test, here I have to set up an ophthalmologist appointment. If I go to a public clinic, it's free but is at least three months' wait. The private clinic can see me immediately, but will cost eighty dollars—or a week's worth of food. I have little choice, so I visit the private doctor, whose studio is in a normal *palazzo* apartment building.

Because the doctor can hardly see anymore, he has a nurse to help him through the exam. I tell them I only need to read through the eye chart, but they insist on a lengthy procedure. After nearly an hour of tests, the last exam con-sists of giving me eyedrops to dilate my pupils. I leave the office unable to focus properly and am nearly blinded when the sun hits me. My oversized Italian sunglasses save me from stumbling into walls.

This new medical document must be notarized, so I print the necessary form off the Internet at a copy shop. To pay the ten cents for the printout, the copy shop clerk has two pages of receipts for me plus a large form I need to sign. "Just for our records," she says.

One of our neighbors in Vicolo Forni recommends a notary to sign my documents. "He's the big man who is often down in Maurizio's bar, Il Cappuccino. You can't miss him because he fills up the bar. He eats and eats and eats everything in sight. He's really a big, big man," he says with respect and perhaps envy that someone can enjoy food so much.

In exchange for two minutes spent notarizing my documents, the notary doesn't want to be paid. When I insist, he says, "Just buy me a drink sometime at Maurizio's bar, OK?"

I finish the bureaucracy for this eye exam that would have taken five minutes in the United States. I bundle the forms into an envelope and now entrust the Italian mail system with the documents that will give us heat, electricity, and water. A month later, my renewed ID arrives; all the Italian documents worked like a charm. When I examine the driver's license, though, I see that the Minnesota Department of Driver and Vehicle Services, who I thought was so efficient, accidentally put my dad's name on my license, not mine.

Luckily, the landlords are kind enough to keep the utilities in their name. The telephone, on the other hand, requires an enormous setup fee and two months of waiting for the hookup.

Friends from Modena can't understand why we rent an apartment and don't buy it instead. "Why would you throw away all that money on rent?" We could never afford to buy an apartment like this, and mortgage payments would easily be triple the cost of our rent. Because most people don't rent in Italy, apartments like ours are available.

When we are finally ready to relax in our apartment, we tempt bad luck. We rearrange the furniture so we sleep with our feet toward the door. "What are you thinking?" Italian friends say. "Only cadavers have their feet toward the door! Do you want to never wake up again?" We've been in the apartment only a week and already have made so many mistakes.

Il Cappuccino

We didn't have a say in choosing the bar we'd frequent. Maurizio's bar, Il Cappuccino, is directly below our kitchen window, and he greets us nearly every time we go in or out of our front door. If we didn't go to his bar, who knows what would happen? Even so, we never go there often enough to make him happy.

Il Cappuccino is the size of a large walk-in closet, but somehow Maurizio has wedged in a couple of tiny tables, a cooler full of chilled Lambrusco wine (not the sweet stuff), and a large counter extending the length of the bar. More than four customers at a time constitutes a fire hazard. This is Italy, though, so at least ten can squeeze in when necessary. Even the exhaust for the fan doesn't fit, so Maurizio rigged it into our stairwell, sending the smell of fresh croissants and coffee up the hall. Maybe this is another of his ploys to get us to stop down more often.

Once you choose your bar, you should avoid being seen at rival cafés. Your bar often represents your political bent—or more importantly, your soccer team. For clues, look for plastic trophies or the little triangular flag with team colors—usually still in its cellophane sheath to protect this sacred symbol. A crumpled copy of the pink newspaper *La Gazzetta dello Sport* lies on the counter and is picked up by almost every customer—male customer, that is. Cheers or sighs erupt as they check last night's soccer scores. Luckily, I can stay neutral to the politics of soccer since I'm a foreigner. However, I can rarely escape the old grudge of why on earth the World Cup was once played in the United States, because everyone is sure the United States is unworthy of inclusion.

Photos of local boys who made good, Enzo Ferrari and Luciano Pavarotti, hang side by side on the tiny wall space of Il Cappuccino. A large Ferrari banner hangs from the TV suspended overhead in a corner, which is switched on whenever a Formula One race or a soccer game takes place. Il Cappuccino instantly turns into a sports bar, and men sit there almost all weekend and watch the games.

Like the piazza, the bar is an essential part of Italian life. Lines of expectant customers wait to partake in the luscious brew, as the *baristi* dressed in immaculate outfits reign over their espresso machines. The bar is the gathering spot for cappuccino and *cornetto* croissants in the morning. At 11 a.m., it's time for a quick caffeine burst. If time doesn't permit pasta, a *panino* will do for lunch. Finally, an *apertivo* drink is required at sundown to prepare the stomach for supper. Kids are welcome in this warm, well-lit place but are rarely served alcohol, not because it's illegal but because most barkeeps wouldn't dare incite the wrath of protective *mammas*. Pure social pressure maintains a drinking age much more effectively than any Italian law could. Instead, the coffee dealers lure the addicts into their impeccable dens and effortlessly prepare their potion.

Drive-up coffee bars are unheard of, and carrying a big mug of coffee in the car is just plain wrong to any Italian. A bottomless cup of coffee sounds like a money-growing-on-trees fantasy, and timers on coffeemakers to start the brewing process would make a mint in Italy if someone invented one for espresso. Coffee is never flavored; after all, coffee is a flavor. Coca-Cola in the morning is like cappuccino after lunch; you just don't do it. If you do, expect one of those disgusted glances from your *barista,* who pities your stomach for this culinary faux pas.

Cantuccini are another point of contention. These almond cookies known in America as *biscotti*—which just means "biscuit" or "cookie"—are supposed to be dipped in sweet Vin Santo, Albana, or Moscato wine. I prefer them in cappuccino, but friends' reactions are immediate, "You dip it in coffee? Che schifo! How disgusting!" Sometimes they try it to be polite and taste it. "Non c'è male. It isn't bad, however, it is incorrect. Just so you know." The protocol around coffee in Italy is strict, and experimenting is left to foreigners.

Coffee comes in many shapes and sizes: *lungo* (long-pour espresso), *ristretto* (short-pour), *americano* (watered-down), *latte macchiato* (milk "marked" with a little coffee), *caffè macchiato* (coffee "marked" with fluffed milk), and *cremino* (Maurizio's specialty with cream and sugar). The legend of the world-famous cappuccino credits the hooded Capuchin monks in their light-brown robes for brewing the first frothed drink. Since *cappuccio* means "hood," each cappuccino you drink is like a small St. Francis of Assisi in your cup. If all these options don't appeal to you, "correct" your coffee with a healthy shot of *grappa* (Italian firewater) for *caffè corretto.*

One morning, I invite a visiting American friend into Maurizio's bar, where she orders three cappuccini back to back. Maurizio waits for the punch line. When she holds up three fingers, he doesn't say a word and furrows his brow while he promptly serves the three cups of coffee. The regulars watch intently as she drinks. They then discuss this strange phenomenon in dialect, saying it's as though she went to Communion and asked for seconds. Maurizio whispers to me, "Voi americani esagerate sempre!" (You Americans always exaggerate everything!).

Only by making these blunders do I understand the unwritten rules of Italian etiquette. After much observation and practice, I crack the code on getting an espresso Italian style. When strolling through town on the evening *passeggiata*, I run into a friend. Custom calls for one of us to offer a cup of coffee. We step into the closest bar—preferably Il Cappuccino if I don't want to hear later about being some sort of traitor. I raise two fingers, and the barkeep understands. He nods, barely moving his head. Choice between a dozen different ways to have coffee is only for the fickle; just gesturing *due* means two espressos; anything else requires actual talking.

Maurizio rarely smiles or speaks when fixing espresso; he must concentrate for perfection. The ritual begins as the *barista* bangs out the old grounds but never washes the coffee machine with soap since the flavor would be compromised. He loads it up with fresh grounds and packs it hard. The steam billows around the machine, and the black elixir dribbles down into a pair of heated *tazze* (cups).

He presents the tiny cups with only a thimble full of espresso lining the bottom. Everyone dumps in at least a teaspoon of sugar, which somehow dissolves in the already thick brew. Stirring the sugar is the longest part of the process and requires an absolutely bored expression, as though each swirl of the spoon might bring its stirrer closer to the grave.

Perhaps this painful anticipation explains why the next step is so quick. One, two, three, boom! Down the hatch! No sipping allowed. The coffee is consecrated, and the caffeine seeps into the veins of the devoted and faithful to their coffee bar. The effect of the drug only exacerbates the struggle of who will pay at the register. Then we're out the door, only to have the ritual repeated when the next friend is encountered.

This ceremony is repeated on every corner of every Italian town, almost as an act of breaking bread to show true friendship. While Italian churches are packed on Sunday, bars in Italy are overflowing every day.

Lord Arnold and the Knight

My fantasy of being a highly paid travel writer by writing columns in the local Italian weekly is shattered when I cash my paycheck of $60—the sum of a month's work. To pay the bills, I convince myself that going undercover as an English teacher will yield great insight into Italian culture and I won't have to compromise my literary dream. After all, even James Joyce taught English in Trieste for eleven years while he was writing *Ulysses*.

My first day of teaching, I realize this is no ordinary school. The name of the school, Lord Arnold, sounds erudite and British, but I can't help but picture Benedict Arnold, the traitor: the name should have tipped me off. The other clue was that the Lord Arnold School offered me a job on the spot and didn't even ask if I'd taught before.

One of the three secretaries says the boss, Signor Truffino, wants to see me immediately for an interview. On the wall of his office are a couple of college degrees in foreign languages (which another teacher later points out he didn't earn; they were given to him by a friend at the university as honorary degrees ten years before). Above them is a framed certificate with gold stamps all over it declaring him a *cavaliere*, or knight. Should I call him "Cavaliere Truffino"?

Whether or not the degrees are valid, Cavaliere Truffino is able to switch languages with amazing fluidity, or at least enough to impress me. He is in his midfifties and has a well-trimmed beard with just a hint of gray, which only adds to his refined look. His smooth silk tie wraps tightly under his stiff collar, but his impeccable suit does not hold back his energetic personality.

He wants me to start immediately, even though I have no formal training in teaching English. "Just talk to them and correct their miserable pronunciation," he tells me disdainfully. He explains that most of the students are high school students or young professionals who need to learn English. He widens his eyes for an unintentional Charles Manson impersonation and declares, "Go in that classroom with an air of confidence. Show them who's boss!" I point to him. He replies, "Grazie. Yes, I am the boss here, but *you* are the boss in the classroom!"

He lets me in on a secret skill he wants me to perfect. "Never let students know that you don't know the answer to a question!" In fact this sums up a common Italian characteristic I'm trying to learn: never let on that you don't understand. Smile and nod or change the subject.

When I ask him how much teachers get paid, he scrawls some unintelligible little graphs on scratch paper about the pay scale and tells me, "You must work! Work, work, work! Then you will make money." He proudly holds up his incoherent graph of the pay scale as evidence of how hard I need to work for him. I assume I'm incompetent, because I don't understand his chart. Then I realize he's teaching me another important lesson: when you can't give a straight answer, confuse them. If they ask for clarification, act exasperated until they become embarrassed and give up.

Cavaliere Truffino finally sets down his scribbles and tells me that in exchange for making me rich through teaching, he asks one thing, "I don't care what you do here. I don't care if you sleep with all of your students; that's fine. I know I would! I just ask one thing of you, one very small thing. When you're lying in bed with your students the next morning, just don't say anything bad about the school. That's all I ask."

Three secretaries shuffle papers busily in the tight reception room of the Lord Arnold office. Giulia, with her bobbed hair and wide smile, always fills me in on the gossip around the office when no one else is around. Although she chats more than anyone else, she also is the most efficient. One of the secretaries, Sasha, from Ukraine, wears skintight jeans and clingy T-shirts and is impatient and talks about all the work she's doing to prove she's indispensable. No one knows much about the computer, but Sasha types like a submachine gun. They don't seem to do much, but the boss likes them. I mean, he *really* likes them.

His wife, Maria, often works in the office, but it's mostly to watch over the situation. The worry lines on her face have stuck. She tries to smile at me when I enter the office, but her thick makeup gives the impression of a frightening scowl. For some reason, she trusts me and assigns me the best teaching jobs.

One evening at 10 p.m., after I finish teaching a late class, the boss is still in his office while Sasha busily types a translation for him. I'm exhausted and want to get home, but he asks me to come into his office. Although I know I have a lot to learn from him, I fear a recap of the lengthy interview of scribbling graphs. When a knight calls, I must answer.

"So, how are you?" Cavaliere Truffino asks. I'm confused, because he usually has no time for small talk. As I prepare to tell him all my problems, the phone rings. The boss politely asks me to excuse him as he angrily bellows into the receiver that he's having a conference. He hangs up and calmly returns to our conversation. The phone rings again. He picks up the phone and says in Italian, "Listen woman, why don't you believe me that I'm having a very important conference with Eric. You don't believe me? Well, here he is!" He hands me the phone to speak with his wife, and I realize I'm stuck providing an alibi for a liaison with the Ukrainian.

He thanks me as I leave, saying, "You know how jealous women get."

After this incident, I'm the boss's temporary favorite. One evening when I get home, the phone rings, and the boss tells me I have to dress up to be a translator for national Italian television. RAI TV will be filming a special live show in Modena's indoor arena tonight. I'm supposed to sit in the RAI radio car, in case the newscasters need an English interpreter for live news from CNN.

In vain I explain to Signor Truffino that I've only translated *written* material into English, never simultaneous speaking into Italian. "Just act like you know what's going on. Hold your head up high, wear nice clothes, and people will believe you." In other words, be *furbo*, or clever, and take advantage of the situation. Meanwhile, he's going to sit up in the VIP section with the other *cavalieri*.

The arena, which is used for basketball games and concerts, now hosts this Italian news talk show with many Italian television personalities that the boss assures me are very, very important. I'm placed out in the mobile news truck in the parking lot with the Italian newscasters. The real reporters from RAI don't catch on that I'm an imposter who would have an awful time being thrust onto live national television to translate the English of CNN into my choppy

Italian. My newscast would interrupt all other programming in Italy and be transmitted across the country as breaking news. Signor Truffino is very proud that one of his own translators will be on national television, but he tells me to make sure that I mention the Lord Arnold School of Modena.

Luckily, no big bombs explode this evening, so I'm paid just to sit in the RAI radio car with the big satellite dish on the roof. The television crew tells me I can make a couple of calls to pass the time, so now I'm being paid to chat on the phone to my friends overseas. I imagine my boss would be proud of me for being *furbo*. Instead, after the show, he doesn't want to pay me, since I didn't have to translate anything. I learn the most important part of being *furbo* is knowing when to keep your mouth shut.

In Italy, the idea that a man would *provarci* (or give it a try) with a woman at work doesn't seem to be frowned on. After all, who can blame you for trying? In the United States, a similar situation is much more risky for men, or as an Italian friend put it, "Sexual harassment? That's just an American thing; it doesn't exist in Italy."

Giulia the secretary tells me about the bizarre situations that unfold at the school, like when my fifty-year-old boss propositioned a twenty-one-year-old American teacher. After an evening class, she bent down to get some papers from a cabinet in the office. He was right above her and sat down next to her to declare: "You're like a strawberry cake and I want to eat you up!" He used a similar tactic when a Welsh teacher bent down to put away some books; he knelt down to kiss her when she wasn't expecting it.

In fact, the boss isn't above giving it a try with any of the young women. He was smitten by a young Irish teacher with a lilting accent. For her birthday, he interrupted her class with champagne and cake. While her students were waiting for the lesson to continue, the boss praised the Irish people as jolly and fun loving and begged the teacher to sing a song. When she refused, he broke into "Amazing Grace" in her honor and moved in to give her a wet birthday kiss.

As ridiculous as these situations are, they're nothing compared to what I've read in the Italian newspapers. When women began being admitted to the military, a journalist (obviously male) was thrilled by the prospect of military-issue brassieres. Drawings depicting these sexy armed women were seen in most newspapers, so men could envision hot dominatrices with M-16s.

In a sexual assault case that made it to the courts, judges ruled that rape is impossible if a woman is wearing tight jeans. The judges let the accused predator off the hook because they deemed that he couldn't have raped the woman with the tight jeans in the front seat of a Maserati, since the sports car is far too small to maneuver to a workable position.

Office etiquette was clarified by another judge, who declared a pat on the butt is OK as long as it's not an "act of libido." A female coworker was interviewed after the ruling. "Keep in mind that it was on *top* of her clothes, really nothing. If it were underneath the clothes, or if he had grabbed her, then it would be something."

When I mention these cases to the secretaries in the office, they agree that the Italian legal system does not protect women. I explain the idea of sexual harassment in the United States, but Giulia says, "You Americans go too far!" Giulia and Sasha agree that they like to be complimented and don't want anything to make men worried about asking them out. "And the kisses! In Italy we like to kiss on the cheeks."

Terror and Courtesy at the Esselunga Supermercato

I'm terrified of little old Italian women. In the crowds at the market, they jab their elbows into my gut as they push their way to the front of the line. These aged tycoons can easily barge through a squadron of large men waiting in line, and no one says a word. Old women can give the evil eye like nobody's business. Surveys in Italy reveal more than half the population believes in this curse. I'm hardly superstitious, but why tempt fate?

If we're invited to an Italian friend's house, inevitably it's the grandmother who scrutinizes how little I eat as she insists on stuffing me silly. When an Italian old woman tells you to eat, you do it. My problem is more serious, though. They always ask me for help.

I'm cursed with having one of those faces that says, "Hello, my name is Eric. May I help you?" Sure, I've tried to look mean—shaved my head, pierced my ears, worn ripped jeans, put on T-shirts sprinkled with profanity, dyed my hair blue—but I can't escape it. I have a service-industry face.

The most dangerous situation for me is the grocery store. Few Italian men, especially young *giovanotti,* set foot in supermarkets. So when I do, old women prey on me for assistance. When I'm not looking, they grab me by the elbow hard and don't let go until I give in to their demands. If I act like a dumb foreigner who doesn't understand them, they glare at me until I help them. They know I'm lying.

One day while out for a stroll, I walk in front of a large supermarket. I don't need any groceries, and I'm not even shopping, but that doesn't seem to make a difference. When I think I'm a safe distance away, a shopping cart jabs me in my calves. I turn around to find an immense woman begging me to push the cart for her and unload it in her car. She describes her hefty build as "pregnant," even though she looks far too old to be making babies.

A bus stops nearby, and I think about hopping on it to escape, but I'm fairly positive she would hunt me down like a dog—or worse yet, she could give me the dreaded evil eye, dooming me and my family for centuries.

Emptying her cart is surprisingly painless. The woman even tells me I can take the shopping cart back and collect the one Euro deposit. I wasn't born yesterday and am not about to be fooled by this apparent benevolence. I know that other women in the supermarket are waiting for me to come back to help them unload their carts as well. I bid the pregnant woman a good birth and give the cart to a young Italian boy on the street—poor soul—who is thrilled at this "easy profit." It's cruel, but someone needs to spread the wealth, and pain.

I put off shopping trips as long as possible to avoid these situations, but fate and hunger can be delayed, not escaped. I submit to my appetite and head to the Esselunga Supermercato to load up for the month. I'm amazed to find the aisles nearly deserted and predict that I can stock up in under ten minutes.

Down aisle three, a couple of confused women compare prices on canned würst hot dogs. They see my service-industry face and call me for help. I quickly dodge around the corner and dash down aisle four toward the register.

Then I see her. She's only four feet tall but tough as nails.

Ageless, in that it's unclear whether she's 75 or 175. Her hands are like grappling hooks reaching out for my elbows. I try to sidestep her to the left, but she matches my move. Then I push my cart to the right and hang a quick U-turn. When I think I'm home free, I notice the two women with the cans of weenies approaching me for help. I turn back around, and she has closed the gap between us. She wields her little shopping cart as a weapon and sinks it into the back of my knees. I stumble and turn to witness her awful toothless grin. I'm trapped.

Then she utters those dreadful words that give me cold chills: "Excuse me giovanotto [young man], can you help me?" I explain that I don't work there, but she just shakes her head as though that's no excuse. Instead, she pulls out an ancient tape recorder and demands my help. "Do you know what size batteries I need for this? I can't believe there are so many different sizes!" I examine the machine and choose the right batteries, but then she tells me to open the package of batteries and put them in the recorder.

I'm worried a real store clerk will nab me for shoplifting batteries but then realize they're probably hiding to avoid these tough old ladies. When I hesitate to open the package, she grabs my elbow and squeezes hard. Pain shoots to my brain, and I'm left with no recourse but to dutifully load the tape recorder with batteries. By that time, the two other ladies have converged on me, holding up their cans of hot dogs with their mouths open ready to ask a question. The battery lady raises her hand and halts them before they can say a word. "No! È mio! He's mine! I saw him first."

She pulls me away by my aching elbow as I explain once again that I don't work there. Then comes her litany of ailments: varicose veins, a black-and-blue bruise down her back, explosive gas . . . I interrupt her gruesome medical symptoms and agree to help her with her shopping. She thanks me by pulling a chocolate bar off the shelf, opening it, and feeding it to me.

We finally arrive at the last item on her list: one light-bulb, but all the packages come in twos. Still believing me to be a store clerk, she asks if it's OK to just take one. I reply, "Sure, why not? If you only need one, why buy two?" She sets my elbow free for an instant to open the package, and I see this as an opportunity to escape. She leaves the second lightbulb wobbling precariously on the shelf as I run for the door. I say "addio" before she can invite me to her house, lock the door, and stuff me full of food. Without any groceries, I slip out of the supermarket doors, hiding my service-industry face.

Foiling the Cheese Thieves

To escape from the abundance of pork fat in my diet, I tour a cheese factory. My editor, Roberto, does public relations for a farming town and offers to lead me around. Modena falls in the official area that is allowed to make Parmigiano-Reggiano, according to government officials, which I call "the food police," but Roberto is not amused. Authentic Parmesan is edible gold and must be made only with the milk from pedigreed red Reggiana cows. I'm told that wheels of Parmesan fill some local bank vaults, as the value of the cheese wheels remains more constant than any currency. Locals often call it *grana*, which refers to a less costly version of Parmesan-like cheese called *grana padano*. Ironically, *grana* is also slang for "money."

One wheel of Parmesan sells for upwards of $500, so I ask the guide at the cheese factory if they've ever had a security problem. His tone turns somber as he tells me about his encounter with the notorious cheese thieves. "One night, burglars broke into our warehouse and filled their truck with wheels of Parmigiano. Millions of Euros of cheese were in the truck headed for the black market. Luckily, as they drove away, the police noticed their license plates were from out of town. The crooks were caught as they were leaving." Then he whispers, "They were from Naples," as if this was to be expected.

Even though I'm in a warehouse with delicious cheese stacked two stories high as far as I can see, the subject of the conversation inevitably changes to pigs. "The leftovers from making Parmesan are given to the pigs. This is what gives prosciutto its special flavor," the guide notes. "Not only are wheels of Parmesan in the bank, but also legs of prosciutto." Even the cheese is somehow related to the pigs in Modena.

Mold Makes a Good Salami Great

Now that my eyes have been opened, I notice this fond-ness for pork everywhere. Modenese photographer Franco Fontana, who shoots photos for the weekly, pieced together photos of ham next to babies, and pork is paired with long-legged models in ironic collages of hungry desire. Another artist painted copies of Michelangelo's, Caravaggio's, and Morandi's masterpieces on legs of prosciutto ham and displayed them at a fancy Milanese restaurant. My editor, Roberto, went to a villa in Tuscany where a mosaic of fresh salami and mozzarella filled an entire room. "It was absolutely beautiful but stunk like crazy!" he recalls.

In Modena, hogs outnumber humans, and even chocolate comes in the form of "chocolate salami." At the deli under my apartment, I notice a jar of pesto and am excited to make spaghetti with this tasty basil and pine nut topping. At home when I open the jar, the sauce has a definite garlic smell but is pure white. I bring it back to the store, and the clerk exclaims almost joyously, "It's lard! It's not pesto Genovese, but pesto Modenese with ground garlic, rosemary, and pig fat, which you spread on tigelle bread. It's our local specialty and absolutely delicious!"

At first, I tell Modenese friends I'm not a big fan of the lard-filled biscuits called *tigelle*. They're shocked, "You haven't had good lard then!" They then take me to a restaurant to eat the best pork fat in town on dry biscuits with prosciutto and grated Parmigiano-Reggiano on top. Only when I surrender and declare how delicious the creamy lard is will my hosts be satisfied and spare my stomach further fat and my heart the cholesterol-clogging lipids.

In spite of protests, somehow all roads lead to pork, and even the master cheese maker insists I visit his friend's nearby salami factory. Despite his eternally busy schedule, Roberto dutifully drives me to his friend, the pork producer. Italians have a word for salami factory: *salumificio*. To any normal Modenese, seeing hundreds of legs of prosciutto curing in every direction is culinary ecstasy, but the seemingly endless walls of severed pig legs makes me nauseous. I feel the blood rushing out of my face and am worried I'm going to pass out from this morbid but tasty site. I take deep breaths, but huge gulps of pork air aren't exactly what the doctor ordered. I try to hide my queasiness, thank them, and walk toward the door to get out into the fresh air. They won't hear of my departure, since I'm the first American to ever visit. I must bear witness to their butchers' fabulous handiwork. I get a second wind as they give me the grand tour of their pork production.

The guide pulls out a sharpened horse bone and jams it into one of the prosciutto legs. "The bones of horses are porous and absorb the flavor of the pork to show if the meat has aged enough." Before I can turn away, he swiftly places the horse bone covered with uncooked pork under my nose and orders me to "inhale deeply and smell if the meat is properly cured." I hold my breath but pretend to be smelling it.

Just when I think the tour is over, we move to the next room. The space is three times the size of the prosciutto curing room and is full of dangling salamis. "Mold and salami are inseparable," the guide informs me as he points to the white mold covering all the pork. He explains this is how they cure salami and in the same breath asks me why it's so difficult to import Italian meat into the United States. I'm no pork expert, but I don't dare tell him the FDA is probably wary of raw meat cured with mold, no matter how good it tastes.

He shows mercy and grudgingly lets me skip the butchering area. We go straight to the tasting room. Although I have a weak stomach for the slaughterhouse, my appetite for prosciutto is insatiable. The tour guide is happy that I like his product. "Our pork is the best in the world," he claims. "The flavor comes from the land, the air, and the pig's diet of the leftovers from making Parmigiano-Reggiano."

Just as I start enjoying the ham and salami, he pushes me further. He offers me a big bite of the fat and commands me, "Taste it. It's the best lard in Italy." I'm hesitant after the tour of the mold-ridden pork products, but I chew the lard to make him happy. My heart slows to a lazy purr from the grease, but the lard is instantly satisfying, as if all the comfort of a pork dinner or leg of prosciutto was condensed into one bite.

"The Poor Meatball!"

I fooled myself that I was going to support Katy by writing for the weekly newspaper and teaching a couple of English classes at Lord Arnold. Even though I've studied Italian and have already lived in northern Italy, Katy steps in and becomes known throughout Modena as the best English teacher around for *bambini* ages four to fourteen.

People on the street ask Katy directions, believing she's Italian, partially because she has a sense of style (compared to my holey jeans and purple socks) but also due to her brown hair. In spite of two years' living in Italy, my blond hair and blue eyes give me away. Within a few weeks, Katy has figured out nearly as much about Italian culture as I did in all my time in northern Italy.

Knowing only a few words of Italian, Katy schedules so many private, well-paid lessons that she has to turn some down. People I meet ask, "Tu sei il ragazzo della famosa Keti?" (Are you the boyfriend of the famous Keti?—they can never quite pronounce her name). Katy consoles me, "I never studied a spoken language, but I did take five quarters of sign language, which helps with Italian."

Her lessons turn out to be more difficult than expected, not because of the kids but the overly protective Italian *mammas*. The bossy mothers regularly phone to yell at her about any schedule changes and then try to make it all better by giving her expensive little gifts. Some of the ultracompetitive mothers won't even pass on Katy's name and number to other moms who want lessons for their kids. After all, how can their kids get ahead if the other *bambini* have lessons with Katy as well? Part of being first is leaving others behind.

Discipline is very important to Italian parents. One mother watches Katy teach and thinks she's being too kind to the children. "You must be very strict with your students for them to learn. It's OK if they start crying. Then you know you're being hard enough on them." After this lecture to Katy on how to be a rigid, humorless teacher with a class of bawling *bambini*, the mother asks, "Do you know the Pokémon song? The kids love to sing this song and play little games."

Apart from dubious pedagogical methods, most of the teaching materials available in Italy are questionable and tend to be very British, even if parents generally want their kids to learn American English. One book with a lesson for first-graders focuses on Scottish pubs: "What sort of drinks would they have? How do you order a pint?"

Katy has only a few decent books, so she's a regular at the photocopy shop. A new law passes in parliament that only 15 percent of any book can be copied at a time, so the woman at the copy shop has me watch out the front door for the photocopy police as Katy makes multiple copies. The shop is right next to the *carabinieri* office, but this police force is busy smoking cigarettes or piling five at a time into their Alfa Romeos to cruise the crowded streets. The copy shop clerk schemes a way to circumvent the law. She tells Katy to come back as many times as she needs to during the day; she just shouldn't risk copying entire books at one session.

Italian is pronounced exactly as it's written, so teaching

English pronunciation to *bambini* is difficult even with the best materials. *High* is pronounced "eeg," "I go to . . . " is read "eegotow," and *I* is said as "hi." Giving kids letter scrambles to rearrange into words inevitably ends with the kids trying to pronounce the mixed-up letters as shown. The kids are generally unconcerned when they say things incorrectly. Little Francesca says, "I'm swearing a cup," rather than "I'm wearing a cap." When Katy explains the difference, Francesca says in Italian, "English all just sounds the same anyway."

Words the kids do understand usually have a different meaning in English. While Katy is teaching two little eight-year-old boys, Mario and Dario, one of them pipes up, "'Baby' means 'bambino'? Can it not also mean 'Hey baby!'" he says looking as sexy as an eight-year-old can while trying to pick up a girl.

Inevitably, her lessons digress to discussions about food, since it's the best way to keep the kids' attention. She encourages her *bambini* to use a dictionary for words they don't know, so plump little Giovanni looks up *bistecca* (beef steak) in the dictionary because it's his favorite food. After mad cow disease hits, however, he likes *cotoletta alla milanese* (breaded pork cutlet) much better.

They love to learn food vocabulary, but she asks me, "Why do they always start giggling when I say the words *piselli* [peas] and *uccello* [bird]?" I tell her these are kids' words for wiener, willy, etc. I explain the subject of ancient pornographic Italian drawings in Pompeii of penises and how this tradition dies hard in Italy.

Sometimes, Katy can barely understand them, like when they say, "I eat a kitchen," rather than "I eat a chicken." She tells me one of the mothers tried out her English on her, "Do you want a snake?" Katy is horrified since she hates snakes.

Then she looks at the *biscotti* and milk and realizes she means "snack." Some of the ten-year-old boys are so coddled that the mothers never weaned them from their baby bottles. While teaching, Katy has to endure talking over sounds of "slurp, slurp, slurp."

To add variety to the lessons, she invites me to teach the class the song "On Top of Spaghetti" (to "On Top of Old Smokey"). When I explain the lyrics, little Mariachiara screams out, "La povera polpetta è finita sotto il cespuglio!" (The poor meatball ended up under the bush!).

Another way Katy keeps them talking is asking about their favorite food. Her plan backfires when almost all of them agree, "The most beautiful food I eat is würstel. The best pizza is with würstel."

She replies, "Hot dogs? With all the great food in Italy you prefer hot dogs?"

After the lesson, she comes to me exasperated. "Look what my lessons have come to! I'm arguing with a bunch of eight-year-olds about the exact definition of 'hot dog.' They correct me that for a würstel to be a hot dog, it must have a bun." With all the fantastic food in Italy, kids are the same as in the United States and are connoisseurs of hot dogs. "Luckily, their *nonna* [grandmother] interrupted and got them back on track and told me, 'Children nowadays just don't understand that *la vita è dura* [life is hard]!"

Rats in the Canals,
Peacocks in the Piazza

While waiting in line at the drugstore, I overhear the pharmacist inform an elderly woman, "I saw your husband today."

"Really? Where was he going?"

"To Piazza Grande."

"I believe it," the woman responds. "He claims he never goes there, but he always ends up there and spends his whole morning talking to his friends. Men are all the same; they all just want to go to the piazza!"

It's difficult to understate the importance of the piazza in Italian life. One day in Modena's Piazza Grande, new electric buses are on display. The next day, schoolchildren show off dozens of dumpsters that they painted with bright pictures to cheer up the city and endorse a clean environment. On March 8, women carry little yellow mimosa flowers through the piazza in honor of the Festa della Donna, Women's Day. Once a year, the classic antique automobile race, the Mille Miglia, blasts down main street. Modena's famous gigantic son Luciano Pavarotti began his benefit concert series "Pavarotti and Friends" in the piazza, but in his last years digressed to operatic duets with the Spice Girls.

The old men gather in Piazza Grande every morning to discuss politics and the fate of the world. If the weather is hot, they stay in the shadows; on cold days, they shift every few minutes to stay in the sun.

Women strut through the square as the men tip their hats and offer a formal *"Buon giorno."* This ceremony takes a dangerous turn, however, as these ultrafashionable Modenese women attempt to cross the beautiful round stones of the piazza wearing sharp high heels and teeter precariously with every step.

The edges of the piazza are filled with classic one-speed, rod-brake bikes, many dating back almost a hundred years and still working. In spite of the care given to clothes and to making a *bella figura,* futzing around through town on a squeaky old rust-bucket bicycle is common. A few of these less fortunate bikes have been left to die. Any useful part has been stripped, but the bike frames are still firmly locked to racks. The police have better things to do than clear out old bicycles.

Next to these racks, a few newsstand kiosks display every magazine, newspaper, or videotape you could ever want. I notice a couple of teenage boys sneaking a peek at some salacious magazines with busty women splashed across the covers as the vendor is busy chatting with the old men.

The centerpiece of the piazza is the stunning Romanesque *duomo,* or cathedral. Reliefs of religious figures grace the front, complete with oversized heads designed to keep the fear of the Almighty alive. Adam and Eve are being banished by an angry god, and Cain is continually bludgeoning Abel with a giant tree branch. Above these scenes is the gorgeous circular window representing the wheel of fortune, which is also the logo on the neck of local Lambrusco wine bottles.

The side door of the church facing Piazza Grande is guarded by the lions of Modena. In spite of the signs warning of severe penalties if anyone dares climb on these marble beasts, adults with bundled-up *bambini* hoist their little ones onto the back of the *micio* (kitty cat), that is if the old men aren't using the lions as a table for a card game of *scopa*.

A metal cast of San Geminiano, the patron saint of Modena, stands on a balcony above this cathedral doorway. The old men play their nickel-ante gambling safely under this balcony out of his view while the long-dead saint keeps watch over the piazza to bless the good and root out transgressors.

Next to the statue of San Geminiano hangs an enormous bone, a good luck charm, but no one can give me a clear explanation of its origin. One Modenese tells me, "It's a rib bone of a whale discovered under Piazza Grande when builders were excavating for the duomo. You know, millions of years ago, this used to be the bottom of the ocean."

"What are you talking about?" his friend interrupts. "That bone is an elephant tusk that was recovered from when Hannibal crossed the Alps to invade Rome!"

In any case, this ancient trophy is another good topic for a discussion, but perhaps not as good as the marble relief above the balcony. A nude woman is spreading her legs for all to admire her privates. Does this symbolize that she gave birth to Modena? Is this Mary Magdalene? Is this the Virgin Mary? Perhaps she's preparing to give birth to Jesus, and what could be more holy than that? Obviously, the youth of Modena could get a glimpse of the birds and the bees if they just went to church.

The doors on the other side of the *duomo* tell the sixth-century tale of the noble King Arthur's quest for the Holy Grail, which, being a non-biblical tale, is an unusual display for an Italian church. Underneath this image of the mystical search is practical advice to local farmers, or *contadini*, about their duties throughout the year. In September, harvest the crops; in October, mash the grapes for Lambrusco; in February, check your balsamic vinegar, and so on.

One door leads to the Piazza Torre, with the statue of Modena's most famous poet, Alessandro Tassoni, who wrote the mock heroic story of the town's struggle with Bologna. The pigeons, however, have no respect for this dead soul and perch on his head, leaving little dandrufflike dollops covering his shoulders.

The statue is dwarfed by the 290-foot Ghirlandina tower, which like any medieval bell steeple has a healthy lean, perhaps to attract tourists from Pisa. No building in Modena can be built higher than this eight-story marble tower. It serves as a beacon to the locals when navigating Modena's tangly streets, where old canals used to run. But mostly, the Ghirlandina rings out the time and is a call to gather to anyone not already in the piazza.

The only competition to the wake-up call of the Ghirlandina is the early weekend rally when someone gets hold of a bullhorn and can't resist waking everyone who lives close to the piazza. "*Sciopero!* Strike! Everyone come to the piazza!" The speaker shouts into the megaphone, making his voice nearly unintelligible.

I soon learn the Italian art of striking is intricate and complex. Not only do unions organize general strikes, but there are often sympathy strikes by related businesses. To avoid a total shutdown of their business, workers will stage a *sciopero singhiozzo,* "hiccup" strike, and just take an hour off to slow things down and have an extra-long lunch.

At school, students look for any excuse to skip some classes, but teachers' strikes, or *sciopero d'insegnanti,* don't let their pupils off the hook. The *professori* go to school anyway since they can't bear not to have their pupils get their homework. The teachers will be on strike but still working. This noble stance forces the administration to eventually give in to the teachers' demands so they don't make a *brutta figura*, or fool, of themselves.

One morning, the bullhorns blare exceptionally early, and the streets are full of bicyclers rolling into Piazza Grande. A famous bike racer with a shaved head is leading a benefit race through town. Apparently, his chances of winning the Giro d'Italia bike race this year are nil, so he's changed his tactics. To win public sympathy for the supposedly unjust accusations of his years of doping, he's taken to supporting good causes and is even being blessed by the Pope. Owing to serendipity like this, I frequently venture into the piazza to find out what excitement is brewing in the city.

On Sunday, the Ghirlandina starts chiming about five o'clock in the evening. Other bell towers clang their bells within five or ten minutes of the Ghirlandina, some later, some earlier, as though reinforcing this call to prayer. More than filling up the *duomo*, however, these church bells toll to call everybody out to the streets for their evening *passeggiata*, or stroll.

The main drag of Modena is the Via Emilia, an ancient Roman road stretching southeast to northwest across Emilia-Romagna from Rimini, on the Adriatic Coast, to Piacenza, just south of Milan. Modenesi parade along *la vasca*, or the tub, which is local slang for going back and forth along the three-block stretch of the Via Emilia near the cathedral.

Sunday is for window-shopping, but potential buyers must peer through the metal grates in front of the store windows because shops are closed on the Sabbath by law. Stores are closed from 1:00 to 4:00 p.m. every day and also on Thursday afternoons to give shop owners a break. At first this schedule was maddening to figure out, but once accustomed to this system, I found it makes perfect sense to take time off rather than work all the time.

When the stores are shut, many people walk beyond the closed-off and crowded Via Emilia. The old palace of the Duke of Este is now the Accademia, a prestigious military academy, which stands out from the quaint Romanesque town with its haughty formality. Guarding the entrance are statues of ancient warriors: one a Roman centurion, and the other a comically noble caveman with a club and ferocious dog. The huge building covers four square blocks, and sections are occasionally open to the public, especially the military museum with wartime booty. As if the Fascist era were just another historical period, Mussolini relics and tributes to Fascist generals still remain on display. A little shop nearby sells Mussolini coffee mugs for nostalgic Blackshirts wanting to reminisce.

On the other side of town, the town museum, the Palazzo dei Musei, sometimes opens on Sundays for the weekly *passeggiata*. Religious art fills the museum, and an early illuminated Bible has hand-colored pictures on nearly every page. The walls are filled with paintings, depicting scenes from tortuous visions of hell to the cruel punishments that await the sinful to close-ups of the circumcision of Christ. An unusual painting features Jesus in limbo, even though the Pope recently declared that limbo doesn't exist.

These numerous illustrations of impending doom don't keep the Modenesi from committing one of the seven deadly sins: vanity. The *passeggiata* is an excuse to get dressed up in one's Sunday best to strut through town. Young and old gather to chat and stroll through the historical center of town. My shoe salesman student Davide explains that Italian even has a verb meaning to prance like a peacock through town, *pavoneggiarsi*. "In Modena," he tells me, "people walk like a *pavone* [peacock] on the Via Emilia to show their beautiful clothes and talk on their cell phones."

"Boy," says a visiting friend from Boston, "People all look so sexy here, not like in America. They just look great!" Another American friend, dressed in sweatpants, isn't so impressed: "Most of the women dress like the high school slut."

No matter, people do look good, if extravagant. The cadets from the Accademia are let out once a week and walk the narrow streets wearing their capes and gendarme-style hats and carrying miniature swords at their sides in scabbards. Officers are allowed to dress down in civvies, which are usually the latest Armani fashions.

I look at my beat-up duds next to these perfect clothes and begin to window-shop myself. When I calculate that maybe I could afford a nice suit on my miserable salary, I realize the wish to conform has seeped into my brain.

Rather than risking the crowds on the Via Emilia, the old men usually stay in the piazza, dressed in their tailored suits and Borsalino hats. They don't give a hoot about the latest fashions and prefer to socialize under the Ghirlandina.

At seven and again at eight o'clock, the bells ring a somber note that it's time to go home for supper. In the piazza, people bid each other *"Arrivederci,"* and head home for some fresh pasta.

I know when I'm old, I want to come to this piazza. I want to watch everyone parade the latest fashions as if it's so very important. I want to see the marble cathedral, which will outlive all of us. I want to walk down the Via Emilia just as the Romans once did and greet my friends on the way to the town square to play a game of *scopa* on the lions' backs. More than the dinner table, the piazza and the *passeggiata* are where Italy comes alive, and I always want to be a part of it.

The Bicycle Thief

Bicycle bells ringing through the streets convinced us to stay in Modena. The town center is roped off to cars, so old one-speed steel bicycles with Ferrari stickers on them stumble over the stone roads. Where bike lanes intersect, special stoplights with little green, yellow, or red bicycles give the right-of-way. Most of the bicyclists ignore the warning lights but look carefully for incoming Maseratis flicking their high beams as they go too fast to stop.

Police will never lower themselves to riding bicycles. Instead Modena's finest, the *poliziotti*, and the military police (who are the butt of all jokes), the *carabinieri*, cram into their Alfa Romeos and speed dangerously through the town center, as only "emergency" vehicles are allowed through these narrow cobblestone streets.

Modenesi without police uniforms religiously ride their bikes. They get their first training wheels as two-year-old *bambini* and will climb on their bikes well into their old age. "My grandfather rode his bike until he was ninety-three years old," my student Serena tells me. "He could barely walk, but he went to the piazza every day on his bike."

My bike breaks constantly, so I search for a bicycle repairman. I find Signor Grassi, an old codger who spends his days lying on the cement in his blue jumper covered with grease. His tiny little workshop is so full of old bikes he can only reach a handful on the edge and only repairs the ones he chains up on the street.

When he pulls out his blowtorch for a little welding on my bike, I keep my distance in case of explosions from his pungent *grappa* breath. I saw the old mechanic driving the previous day to his workshop. I jumped on to the sidewalk to avoid any sudden swerves from his Fiat, but he seemed to handle himself quite well behind the wheel. Now, here I am entrusting him with my bicycle.

Since I'm a foreigner, he always grumbles to me about how corrupt the government in Rome is. "Ladri! They're all a bunch of thieves!" I understand that he's protesting against those Roman bureaucrats by not paying taxes when he doesn't give me a receipt for my payment; he keeps two sets of books. A policeman also is waiting to get his bike fixed, and I'm sure the repairman doesn't give him receipts for the tiny amount of money he charges. After all, no one else in Modena wants to lie on their back on the sidewalk, elbow deep in oil fixing a bicycle or three-wheeled Ape car, which means "bee" and is the big brother of the Vespa, or "wasp." Why would the government want to stop him from working? If he wants, he can refuse to fix any more bicycles and probably bring the town to its knees.

Since he likes to chat with me, he tells me to check back and maybe he'll fix my bike sometime soon. In the meantime, I buy some tools and repair it myself.

Friends in Modena are astounded that I do simple repairs to my bicycle, such as grease the chain or attach a bicycle bell. When I offer them the spray can to lubricate their rusty, clunking chain, they say, "I'm not a mechanic! I know nothing about bicycles." Perhaps they want to keep him in business.

Right after I fix my bicycle, it's stolen. I nearly lose my job since I can't get to my lessons, and visions of destitution from *The Bicycle Thief* whirl through my head. My friend Marina takes me to the *questura* to file a *denuncia*, or claim. Unfortunately, it's a different office from where my acquaintances work, and the policemen are casually unhelpful. The annoyed paper pusher puts the form I fill out onto a huge pile of dusty documents and hands me a receipt. I ask him when I should expect to hear something. He looks at me, confused. "Oh, we rarely find stolen bikes. I mean look at all these denuncie we have to deal with," he responds, pointing to the precarious stack of paper. "Who has time to look for a stolen bicycle?"

Marina grabs my arm to pull me out of there and thanks the policeman. "What we have to do is just keep going back every week or so and ask about your bike," she explains. "Hold on to that receipt. Eventually, they'll let us look through the old bikes they've recovered in the back and just choose one."

"So this is sort of a bike swap?" I ask.

"Sure, you might even get a better bike. That's why you should always describe your bike as better than it is," she advises. "When you're on the street, though, carry a bike lock with you. If you see someone on the street with your old bike, they'll probably tell you, 'I paid twenty Euros for it, so you have to pay to get your old bike back.' It's stupid, but that's just how it works."

Even though I'm keeping my eyes open for my bike, I need to buy another one—probably a "used" one for twenty Euros. I just hope the person I buy it from isn't on the run from the old owner. Otherwise, I'll be accused of stealing it, but maybe I'll at least get my twenty Euros back. Owing to the thieves, everyone seems to be riding someone else's stolen bicycle, making everyone an accomplice.

I imagine riding a bicycle in Modena is easier than riding

a scooter in Rome but realize there's a certain art to cycling in the city. Here's what I've learned:

1. *Chaos theory in action.* In America, we drive on the right side of the road; in England, they stay on the left side. In Italy, you have your choice. I've had many near accidents on my bicycle when I've tried desperately to stay on the right side of the road. An old-timer actually stopped his bike in front of me rather than let me stay on the right. My orderly world is thrown upside down, as riding on the bike paths becomes an impromptu game of chicken.

2. *The art of giving a buck.* Growing up on bicycles makes acrobats out of Modenese kids, who stand on the back rack and reach down to hold the shoulders of the bicycle driver. The more timid sit on the hard rack and are punished for their cowardice by the gaping potholes. If a guy gives a buck to a woman wearing a skirt, she's enclosed in his arms sitting sidesaddle on the cross bar. The ultimate lovers' test, however, is for the passenger to sit on the handlebars facing the driver. This requires complete trust—but also facilitates mobile smooching.

3. *Holding hands while biking.* When cyclists go side by side on their own bikes, holding hands should only be attempted by the bravest of lovers since each of them can use only one of their brakes.

4. *Hitching a ride.* Tired of pedaling? Just grab on to your buddy on a Vespa and try to hold your bike steady while zooming along at thirty-five miles per hour. Dangerous and surely illegal, but holding on to a scooter leaves any pedestrian in the dust.

5. *The battle of the umbrellas.* Maybe you need to be born in Emilia-Romagna to master the art of carrying an

umbrella while bicycling during the rain. Since medieval times, they have practiced on horses with their lances to spear their rivals. The sly Modenesi probably figure I'm too easy a target to joust off my bike. A gust of wind tries to lift my umbrella as I flail around to keep my balance. My other hand is pumping at the wet brakes to stop before I narrowly miss plowing over some children.

6. *Don't worry about cars.* The first time I pedaled down Via Emilia, the old Roman road that is Modena's main street, cars nearly gave me a heart attack when they zoomed by inches away. The old ladies in their minks slowly pedaling their bicycles ignore all the Ferrari Testa Rossas that double the speed limit, swerve in front of cyclists, and don't hit anyone (usually).

7. *Don't waste time fixing your bike.* Many of the old rod-brake bicycles were used by Italian resistance partisans during the war to battle the Nazis. If you clean up one of these classic old bikes, somebody's going to rip off your museum piece. Besides, if the chain and wheels aren't lubricated, they make more noise, so cars hear you coming. Potential bicycle thieves ask themselves who'd want a piece of junk like that?

8. *Fit the whole family on the bike.* Put one kid in the little seat in the front, one on the bike rack in back, and if there's still room in the basket, give the lapdog a lift.

9. *Never muss up your hair with a helmet.* With so many laws on the books in Italy, politicians in Rome passed another one, requiring helmets for scooter riders, but left bicyclists untouched. Only babies and Mormons risk bad hair days by wearing a bicycle helmet.

10. *Lock your bike up well, and be careful where you leave it!* With a hefty, oversized chain to lock my bike, everyone

in Modena tells me I have a lock for a scooter, not a bicycle. Two of my bikes were stolen when I used a little chain. Now thieves can't cut the chain, but they continue to dismantle and steal the bike pieces. Finally I understand that besides just securing my bike with an oversized lock, I must park it in front of a little statue of the Virgin Mary. Not even thieves risk the wrath of the Madonna, protector of bicycles!

Treachery and Treason amid the Subcommittee of Vespa Paint

In Italy, motor scooters are not just inexpensive transportation or kitsch artifacts. As with many things Italian, scooters are another reason for a good argument.

I have an old Lambretta scooter back in Minnesota, so I decide to accept the invitation to infiltrate the weekly meeting of the Vespa Club d'Italia, which takes place in a Vespa-crazed insurance agent's office (the location seemed all too convenient for him to also acquire new clients). Ten *Vespisti*, Vespa aficionados, are already in attendance, although they bemoan having to meet in the front office while in the prestigious back room the Moto Gilera club is holding its gathering for their much larger, more expensive motorcycles. More horsepower, more pull.

I am introduced to the club members, all of whom have illustrious titles and ranks in the hierarchy; only a handful are simply "members." These ranks are essential to note: the VIPs are those respected enough to be allowed to talk uninterrupted.

Although the club is desperate for new members, they suspiciously ask me what I want. I flatter them, saying I have ventured all the way from the United States just to report on one of their famous meetings. They buy this statement wholeheartedly, proudly replying that people often come from all over the world to consult with them. When asked for specifics, they are a little vague, but they point to one of their members, who recently returned from a Piaggio business conference in Rio; he produces photos of himself arm in arm with two towering Brazilian dancers. These snapshots are passed around to a chorus of "Ooh-la-la." These catcalls are interrupted by Gino, who rhetorically asks, "Have we come here to talk about women or scooters?"

There is no dissent to this logic, and Gino announces the first order of business: the absolute, dire necessity of charting the correct green paint finish of the early Vespas. It has come to his attention that some early Vespas are slightly more metallic looking than others.

The insurance agent interrupts him to talk about an upcoming scooter rally, which causes Gino to raise his voice, demanding that if Vespisti the world over want the "correct" finish, the club must form a Subcommittee of Vespa Paint staffed by experts who will determine exactly the right shade for all restorations.

This is countered by one of the younger members, who states that he personally may not know about paint but he does know all the brake specifications of every Vespa model—not just the early ones.

This statement outrages Gino, who demands no one change the subject from paint. Next week, they can discuss brakes all they want and even form a Subcommittee of Vespa Brakes. Now is the time to talk paint.

Signor Rossi interrupts, opining that instead of forming exclusive committees, wouldn't it be better to teach younger Vespisti the joys of restoring early Vespas? Gino is on his feet, insulted to the core, insisting that if the club designate certain members as experts in specific fields, they will have to learn every last bit of information on that topic and then others can never question their word.

A younger member boldly replies that Gino just doesn't want anyone to question him when he talks about paint. This obvious statement infuriates Gino, and he bangs his fist on the desk. Alas, he can't be heard over the din of argument. Signor Rossi then says they need to ask their president, who is already an hour late (as usual, apparently). In the meantime, they all turn to me, asking what the proper procedure should be: disseminate the valuable information or consolidate it within subcommittees.

After all the shouting, the silence is painful, especially under the hard stare of all eyes. I fidget in my seat and can feel the sweat running down my neck. Have they aimed the lights at me as well? And then the moment arrives: I confess that I don't even have a Vespa. I have a Lambretta scooter and therefore hail from the rival Lambrettista camp.

The silence turns to shock. I'm afraid for my kneecaps and certain that I've lost my chance of ever achieving a prestigious title in the Vespa Club d'Italia. But then Signor Rossi, ever the kind ambassador, reassures me, saying, "Well, actually Lambrettas are better scooters: more powerful, steadier, and two seats."

The room reverberates with outrage. How could one of their own Vespisti prefer Lambretta to Vespa? A traitor in their midst! Treason! Besides, the insurance agent insists, even if Lambrettas are more powerful, there are six times as many Vespas as Lambrettas!

Before lines are drawn and knives pulled, the president miraculously appears. The grave dilemma of the Subcommittee of Vespa Paint is posed to him, and a fuming silence reigns awaiting his decree. He calmly ignores the question and begins telling about the phenomenal soccer game he has just seen: his team won! The insurance agent and several others are incensed. His team is terrible! They didn't deserve to win! The insurance office booms with screams. In the midst of it all, I grab my coat and run for the door as Gino pounds his fist and yells that they are not to change the subject from paint.

Norman the Conqueror

Signor Truffino announces to everyone at Lord Arnold School that we have a new head teacher who will oversee all the English-language teachers. Neil hails from California and has a laid-back can-do attitude. On his first day at the job, Neil and I walk to the bar next to Lord Arnold School for an espresso. He tells me that before this job, he was living in the Italian resort town of Rimini, "doing research on hallucinogenics for my thesis at the university."

"This teaching thing is a temporary gig since I'm really a filmmaker," he boasts. "I just needed a break from the stress of the biz for a while." His Italian students are impressed, which in turn impresses Signor Truffino because Neil can take charge of the classroom. Neil has never taught but impresses the boss with his ambitious bragging. Later I'm told he only worked once on a film set, holding lights and microphones for a TV advertisement.

Signor Truffino and Neil often call meetings of all the teachers so they can give speeches on pedagogy to inspire us. The boss tells all the teachers of Italian that they're dispensable because "any Italian can teach Italian" to the few foreigners in town. They are obviously upset he doesn't recognize their value. To make his point, Signor Truffino gestures toward his wife, Maria, sitting next to him and says, "My wife, for example, doesn't speak Italian very well, not nearly as well as I do, and even she could learn how to teach." I'm shocked that he would dare insult his wife in public, but she nods sadly.

Neil, the head teacher, takes over the meeting to avoid any protests. He steers the topic toward education by claiming, "Spelling isn't really important in English, so we don't need to teach it. Everyone has spell-check on their computer anyway." I suggest that we aren't using computers in the classroom, and the word has to be close enough for the computer to recognize it.

Neil shrugs off my pessimism, and Signor Truffino can't understand all of the English spoken. The boss just pats Neil on the back and motions for him to keep going. Since Neil's grammar lecture was questioned, he begins a history lesson of our language. "English is basically just French because of Norman the Conqueror," he proclaims and writes the name on the whiteboard.

Another teacher politely corrects him that it was "William," not "Norman," and French is actually very different. Neil waves off the criticism as unimportant. Along with the other teachers, I daydream through the rest of the staff meeting.

Luckily, Neil doesn't teach many classes and is mostly in charge of computers. Somehow he's able to convince the boss to have students work on computer-aided instruction in English and phase out the fuzzy, antiquated videotapes from the 1970s. Students have been protesting the staticky videos, so Neil reasons they'll be much happier spending a full hour in front of the computer. This way, real live teachers can eventually be phased out altogether, and think of how much money can be saved! Signor Truffino compliments him on the plan and gives him a raise.

Neil and the boss have the same business philosophy, and their taste for women extends to the same Ukrainian secretary, Sasha. When the boss isn't putting in late hours at the office, Neil is. Even the other secretary Giulia isn't sure if they've discovered their mutual affairs, or if they would even care. Regardless, the teachers tiptoe around the topic, and the boss's wife increases her scrutiny.

Until the computer system can be completely enacted, the Lord Arnold School still needs new native-English-speaking teachers. Neil posts ads on the Internet and asks anyone interested (preferably females) to send a photo. Tapping into the romantic weakness of Americans and Brits desiring to live in Italy, he keeps a steady supply of young women applicants.

One of the new teachers comes to Modena in search of relatives but has no specific contacts. She finds the phone number of some people in Modena with her same last name, and they're thrilled she is coming to visit from America. The whole time she stays with them, no one is ever sure if they're actually related. Both parties trace back their ancestry but never find any relatives. In the end they reason there's no relation. They enjoy each other's company, so it doesn't seem to really matter.

The head teacher's plan to bring in young women backfires, however, when they accept Grace, a cute, friendly, but inept, teacher from the United States. The school is putting her up in a Stalinist-looking high-rise with four other teachers, including the Ukrainian secretary, Sasha, who can't stand her. Having never lived away from her family in her small town in rural Kansas, Grace isn't used to living with roommates, turning off the lights when she leaves, or shutting the bathroom door when using the toilet. Most of her habits, like asking her roommates to pray with her in her room, don't endanger anyone's life, however. Other quirks—like

leaving the unlit gas burner on full for an entire evening—
are less endearing.

In an attempt to make friends, Grace willingly hands
out her phone number and address to a couple of mysterious Moroccans hanging out at the train station. Luckily, the
more savvy Sasha won't let them in. Somehow, Grace's pray-
ing pays off, protecting her in Modena.

In spite of being in the land of some of the best food in
the world, the other teachers tell me that Grace survives
on chocolate bars and a huge pineapple cake that has been
sitting out on the counter for weeks. The other roommates
aren't much better. They open tins of canned beef, turn
them upside down on a plate, and dig into the gelatinous
meat still in the cylindrical shape of the can.

The other roommates and I convince Grace to cook pasta
to round out her diet—this is Italy after all. She makes one
big batch of penne with red sauce from a jar, which lasts for
three weeks. She never refrigerates it but leaves it in the pan
on the counter. When she's hungry, she heats it up and eats
some of it right out of the pan. The smoke alarm is un-
plugged since her pasta burns to the bottom when she for-
gets it on the stove during her prayers. When the blackened
noodles are all gone, she throws away the scorched pan. She
thanks me for suggesting that she make pasta, as she starts
over with a new batch and new pan.

For some reason, the school entrusts Grace with one of
their cars to drive all the teachers to the lessons at a company just outside of town. One day, she shows up late in the
car, thus holding up all the other teachers as well. "Grace,
where have you been?" Neil asks, worried that all the lessons have now been delayed.

"Oh, shopping," Grace giggles. "I know I really shouldn't
since I don't have much money, but I can't resist."

While waiting for a hole in the traffic to enter a busy road, she sees a break and guns the engine. Unfortunately, a car still in front of us is waiting to enter as well. We smash full force into its rear. Grace apologizes and takes down the driver's name. Most of the dents are to the bumper of the school's car, and the man whose car was hit mostly wants to ask Grace out on a date. He tells her not to worry about his car and writes down his cell phone number for her. When we return to the school, she nonchalantly hands off the phone number to Neil and tells him she got in another accident (her second).

For a month, Grace doesn't have another accident, but then one day she disappears. With one of her roommates, she goes to the town of Trento in the Alps on a chartered bus from Modena. Every year, shoppers from all over northern Italy go to an enormous Christmas market in this quaint mountain city. When the bus is set to come home in the evening, Grace is gone, and the roommate has no idea where she is. The busload of elderly people—some with canes and walkers—scour the market calling for her. After more than an hour of searching, they leave and return to Modena. We all fear the trusting Grace has been abducted, but the school doesn't want to call her parents or the police—perhaps they want to avoid any run-in with the law.

Two days later, Grace waltzes back into the school as if nothing has happened. Everyone breathes a sigh of relief and tells her they feared she was kidnapped or dead. She says, "Oh, didn't I tell you I was going to spend a few nights there?"

I don't know if this is the final straw, or if it is the third accident with the blown-up car engine, but the school fires Grace. Within a week, she finds a job at a different school.

While Sasha and her roommates are relieved that Grace

has moved out, the replacement tenants aren't much better. A woman and her nineteen-year-old daughter from Calabria sublet Grace's room. The mother smokes cigarettes all day and watches soap operas, while the daughter has an affair with the fifty-seven-year-old landlord. The roommates miss Grace's high jinks compared to their new depressing companions. One of the English teachers in the apartment tells me, "At first the landlord's affair with a teenager bothered me, but then I thought 'Oh well, it's Italy.'"

Eat Your Hat, Cowboy

Nowadays, the only hats worn regularly have been relegated to sports and war, baseball caps and helmets. Perhaps a couple of exceptions would be the occasional appearance of hats on the heads of the trendy or the cold. I remember refusing to wear a hat during a Minnesota blizzard and warming my ears with my gloves, risking frostbite to stay "cool" on my way to high school.

In Italy, I figure I can fit in with my new hat since the old men in the town square never leave home without their hats. Bums and street musicians still pass their hat for tips and alms, and even hipsters put on big Russian fur hats to warm their ears and snub animal rights activists.

Owning a hat is a responsibility in Italy. Hat protocol is strictly enforced through rigid unwritten rules: hold your hat in your hand upon entering the cathedral in respect to the Almighty; remove your cap when another poor soul meets his maker and the funeral party marches to the cemetery plot; hang your hat before pulling up to the table unless you want *la mamma* to smack you with a spoon; and God forbid tossing your hat on the bed unless you have a death wish!

I finally broke down and bought a knockoff of the classic Borsalino hats. I've wandered by the hat store a block from my house many times admiring the array of old-style hats, especially the expensive Borsalinos, which are essentially an

Italian Stetson. I've been wearing my heavy Minnesotan wool ski cap, and curious Italians constantly want an explanation. After all, I'm not on the ski slopes so what on earth am I thinking? My St. Paul Saints baseball cap makes them think I'm on my way to play "the most confusing sport ever invented."

Entering an Italian hat store is a step into the past, as Americans have given up wearing hats ever since JFK went hatless at his inauguration. I'm sure Kennedy took a cue from my fellow Minnesotan Charles Lindbergh, who took off his ski cap (or was it an aviator's helmet?) after his flight landed in Paris. The money saved on hats in the United States has since been spent on getting the proper hairdo at the barber.

In Italy, the hat still makes the man, even though it's mostly the older men. The clerk at the store is happy to pull out a dozen different styles of hats, even though I know exactly which one I want. There's the Jackie Stewart model, the Greek fisherman's hat, the Basque beret, etc. Finally, she lets me try on the version I've admired in the window. It's made of the skin of *lepre,* which I find out is hare, not leper.

My American friends greet me with "Hey, mafioso!" when they see the hat, probably expecting me to be munching a toothpick and tossing a silver dollar in the air to complete the look. For the most part, hats in the United States have been put into cold storage and are only pulled out for comedians to poke fun at foreigners: a tilted beret on the head with a baguette under one arm is a snooty Frenchman; a perfectly groomed bowler accompanied by a three-piece suit and a cane implies an uptight, but practical, Brit; and a feather poking out of a green Tirolean hat means a jolly beer-guzzling Bavarian with lederhosen. A hat becomes a jab at those people a little different from ourselves: Napoleon's sidewise general's hat means another cuckoo has cracked; a proud dude sporting a ten-gallon Stetson leads to whispers of "all hat and no cattle"; and a maroon fez with a gold tassel is a sure sign of a Shriner on a scooter.

Wandering into the piazza one day with my fake black Borsalino with the small brim, I figure I can sneak in to watch the old men play their Italian card game *scopa* on the back of a scooter seat. They eye me quizzically as though to say, "Who the heck does this giovanotto [young man] think he is in that hat?" They don't seem to mind as long as I'm not an undercover cop trying to bust their petty gambling.

Afterwards, I hop on my bike as the fog starts rolling down the streets on this chilly evening. A couple of Italian high schoolers laugh at me, and I assume they think I'm making a clever spoof of the old men and their hats. They surprise me when they mix up their stereotypes, yelling, "Hey, Tex! Ciao, Americano!" Apparently, the hat doesn't make me a mafioso in Italy, only a dude dressed like a cowboy. I greet them in English, and they realize that I actually am American. Or maybe they can't hear a word I say since they are too busy trying to warm their ears with their gloves.

Later, when the clerk from the hat store sees me walk by, she tries to lure me inside thinking I'm a regular customer. I tell her that the old men in the piazza look at me as if I'm crazy. She shakes her head, "No, no, no. You must have a proper hat for every season and every outfit." So this is how the Italian hat business has stayed booming.

A Night at the Opera

I grew up listening to punk rock—Sex Pistols, Dead Kennedys, Jodie Foster's Army, etc.—so I thought it might take a while to appreciate the highest Italian art form. I was wrong.

My only real exposure to opera was through cartoons of Bugs Bunny as "The Bunny of Seville" or Elmer Fudd singing his heart out to "Kill da wabbit!" over Wagner's cascading orchestral score. Perhaps opera can be funny after all—imagine if Pavarotti could have fit into a bunny suit! Living in Pavarotti's hometown, Katy and I have to experience opera firsthand.

Roberto, my editor, assigns me to write about the new opera production at the recently renovated Teatro Comunale. I'm not thrilled to put on a suit and polish my shoes for a stuffy evening, and even consider bringing a pillow since I might as well be comfortable while dozing.

Entering the lobby of the Teatro Comunale, Katy and I see this high-class crowd is not a bunch that appreciates slapstick. The women are having a bizarre contest to see who can expose the most skin while carrying the most weight—in the form of gold and diamond jewelry—on painful six-inch-high heels. I wonder why the thieves in Modena bother with beat-up old bicycles.

Although it's amusing to watch these top-heavy, weighted-down women on their stiltlike stilettos, the bells announce the overture, so Katy and I struggle to find our seats. I feel surrounded by a pack of wild animals because of all the fur coats—in spite of it being fifty-five degrees outside.

The overture of Giuseppe Verdi's *Otello* begins with a bang. Some of the spectators seem to be sleeping during the slow pieces, but they have just shut their eyes to feel the emotion of the music more deeply.

In the old days, curtains used to enclose the box seats for lusty lovers to take advantage of the most exciting movements—perhaps opera isn't as different from rock 'n' roll as I imagined. I hear operatic performances often lose spectacular amounts of money even if the house is packed. This is like punk concerts, which rarely earn any money, and the rockers who put on the show do it for love of the music. Even the plots of the operas aren't very different from the real lives of rock stars. Verdi's masterpiece *Otello* brings to mind the Sex Pistols. Othello stabs Desdemona, thinking she was unfaithful, and turns the knife on himself—just like Sid Vicious, the Sex Pistols' bassist, knifed his girlfriend Nancy and then himself with a heroin needle.

During intermission, the singers are judged, highlights are discussed, and names are dropped. I overhear an opera buff in a silk ascot proclaim he prefers Spanish singer Placido Domingo to Pavarotti, a statement tantamount to treason in Modena. "Domingo is more versatile and has a wider range," the man proclaims a bit too loudly. "Pavarotti is past his prime!" A perturbed woman wrapped in a mink confronts the turncoat, exclaiming, "Go to Spain then!"

They remain mostly civil and reach a compromise that nobody sings "Nessun Dorma" from *Turandot* better than Modena's fat man. I want to add that Pavarotti sang with the Spice Girls, but shouldn't he have sung with Johnny Rotten instead? I don't think they'd understand.

At the end of the show, the audience gives the verdict. Italians scream *"bravo!"* and *"bis!"* (encore) for an extraordinary performance and aren't afraid to whistle and boo bad singers right off the stage.

Because of the lack of other live music in Modena, we start going regularly to the opera. Mozart's opera *Idomeneo* is a smash, with timpani filling the theater when Electra falls on the floor and screams in rock 'n' roll ecstasy. Now I understand why ol' Wolfgang dyed his hair blue: to shock.

Then comes Strauss's *Salome,* with royal guards stabbing themselves when they see Salome's erotic dance and John the Baptist's head carried on a platter. This is truly demented material, far worse than the punk music that carries a label warning of adult material. How can people fall asleep?

Four, Five, Sex . . .

One of my classes at Lord Arnold is composed of four middle-aged women who all speak at the same time. Somehow they can listen to the three other women chattering away and add their own comments simultaneously. I admire the cognitive ability of these women to process and produce at the same time. I was raised never to interrupt and to let others finish, but think how much time could be saved if we could all process what others say while we speak ourselves. Besides, if you don't interrupt in Italy, you'll never speak. In fact, I don't speak much with them, and when I do, I'm not sure they can actually hear me. This is fine. I'm paid for an hour of just listening like a therapist, and they're having a grand old time in their English lesson.

During one of these lessons, one woman pinches my cheek and says, "If I were just a little bit younger, mmm, who knows how much fun we could have together? But I'm too old, aren't I?" At first I'm frazzled, but I assume it's a compliment to have women significantly older than my mother propositioning me. Usually when older people tell me how old they are, I reflexively respond, "Oh, you're not so old!" But with these women, I don't dare.

I resort to teaching them something simple: English numbers. Even this is challenging since they repeat "one, two, tree, four, five, sex . . . " After a few times, I point out that it's "six," not "sex," and explain the meaning. The women jokingly act shocked and tell me, "You naughty boy, we should spank you! You behave now!"

My favorite student is Davide, a young executive for a big shoe company, who wants to learn as much street talk as possible. When I'm not careful, he picks up any slang that slips out of my mouth during our one-on-one lessons. With the help of his dictionary, he pieces together expressions that are shocking to hear from a foreigner. My boss, on the other hand, assures this important client that we teach the "Queen's English," not American slang. But as soon as Signor Truffino is out of the room, Davide says, "I shit my trousers! He is big ball breaker, no?"

Although Davide wants to learn to be a slick speaker of street slang, his odd use of grammar is so endearing that I can't bring myself to correct him. Assuming I'm homesick, he asks, "You feel like to ride scooter at lake and forest, yes?"

Davide is my star student because he needs to learn English to advance in his job at the shoe company. He brings magazines into class that are far too difficult for him. He dutifully underlines every word he doesn't understand, so essentially every phrase of the magazine is highlighted. The only words that stick in his memory are slang—"cracker," "I got game," "hip," and so on. To ask if we should take a break he says, "You dude, Eric, you want that we chill out?"

He's been studying hard to get ready for a big dinner meeting with three American colleagues in Bologna. After this meeting, he tells me he couldn't understand a word the Americans said because they had their mouths full the entire evening. From then on, we eat snacks during the lessons so he can understand Americans chewing.

Most students want to learn formal business English, but trying to correct their pronunciation so they avoid making gaffes is difficult. In Italian, the *h* sound doesn't exist, so my students inevitably overcompensate by adding *h*'s to every word that begins with a vowel, and then forgetting them when they're written. For example, "I am" becomes "Hi ham!" My name, Eric, is essentially unpronounceable and becomes everything from "Harry" to "Henry" but usually ends up sounding like "headache."

Vowel sounds are a trick for Italians as well. During an evening lesson, one of my students asks me, "Is it right to say when I call a client, 'Please turn on your fux machine'?" I try to correct her pronunciation, but it doesn't quite work.

I say, "Fax."

She says, "Fux."

"Fax."

"Fux."

I choose a different tack and explain that we also use "fax" as a verb. That only makes the situation worse. She responds, "Oh, you use 'fux' as verb? So when I call on the telephone to a client I can say, 'I want to fux you'!"

I steer students away from certain words that can lead to these embarrassing situations, but it's usually worse to point out these pitfalls. One evening while my students are writing a little essay, one woman asks me quietly, "Do you have a rubber we can use?" I blush beet red but then realize she wants an "eraser" and had learned the British word for it. The class bursts out laughing when I explain the difference. The lesson is sidetracked, so I try to calm them down by telling them about English-speaking tourists who come to Italy and ask in stores if their food has *preservativi* in it.

They look at me appalled at how sick we are. One

student searches in his dictionary and asks, "Why do you Americans want food with 'prophylactic' inside?" I explain that the English word *preservatives* actually means *conservanti* in Italian.

This leads to the discussion of "How do you say *preservativo* in English?" "Condoms!" yells the woman who asked me for a rubber. The whole class looks at her, surprised that she knows the answer. "Well, I've just heard that," she continues, embarrassed. "I never use them though."

To stop her from putting her foot farther into her mouth, I try to change the subject, but the class now wants to learn some profanity. Just then, the boss peers through the little window into the classroom and sees all the words on the board. He gives me a thumbs-up.

Lessons from Guido

I never have much luck with the Italian mail system. One day when I bring a postcard into the post office, the mailman tells me I have to pay more because there are too many words on it. Not understanding how this could make the slightest difference, I ask him, "Why?" He looks at me as though I'm being belligerent and trying to cause trouble. "Because the postcard now weighs more," he responds in all seriousness as the impatient people behind look at me annoyed. I'm shocked at this logic. He truly believes an extra bit of ink causes the letter to weigh more. My arguing is futile, so I pay the extra thirty Euro cents.

Whenever I mail anything, I'm resigned to the fact there's a decent chance it will never arrive. When I send priority mail overseas, the receiver sometimes gets it mangled and placed in a little plastic bag with a curt note of explanation. The shape of the letter was incorrect, or a corner was hanging out, so the post office workers hold themselves blameless that it got eaten by some enormous machine.

I spend $50 to send some of my writing via insured international express mail to a publisher in the United States. My editor calls once he receives the package and asks if I'm angry with him. As though cursing me for not being willing to risk regular noninsured airmail, the post office delivered the now dog-eared package in the usual plastic bag, but this time filled with rodent excrement.

I subscribe to *Time* magazine, mostly out of curiosity to see if the magazine will actually make it to my door. When the mailman finally gets around to it, he delivers copies of *Time* in a bundle of five issues of "current" news from the last month with a little postcard to send back to the magazine's headquarters asking if the issue arrived. The logic escapes me. Even if the magazine makes it to my mailbox, chances are the postcard won't make it back. And how many people bother to mail the postcard back?

In spite of my experience, I'm careful not to complain openly about the mail service, because most of my Italian friends will defend the postal system out of a feeling of national pride. (Yet I notice many of them send their letters as registered mail to improve the chances of delivery.) Complaining only risks the mailman finding out about my dissatisfaction and further delaying my postal service.

Mail scandals are often splashed across the front page of Italian newspapers. Considering the Italian postal enterprise is larger than the entire Italian railroad system, there's bound to be a few underpaid and corrupt mail carriers. Following a lengthy postal strike, a few of the post offices were so clogged with stacks of mail they knew they would never be able to catch up, so old letters were supposedly burned or bundled and sold to a German recycler. With stories like this, I should be thankful mail arrives at all, even if it is mangled.

Knowing the postal system's shady reputation, I enter the central post office in Modena with skepticism. Plaster is falling on sheets of plastic draped overhead as *muratori* (wall builders) are busy hacking away at the cement to renovate the building.

I have a frog umbrella to mail my three-year-old nephew

in Minneapolis. The laid-back guy at the counter looks at the package, reads the address, and says in English, "Oh, Minnesota! I have a girlfriend in Minnesota!"

He introduces himself as Guido. He wants to visit Minnesota, but I warn him about the subzero winters that are so cold the lakes freeze. He assumes I'm joking. He's from the south and can't imagine a winter colder than northern Italy's. I stupidly suggest he's like *il postino* from the movie since he's from Naples, but he patiently corrects me that he is not a lowly "mailman" but an *impiegato della posta* (postal employee).

I stop by the post office often to mail letters and chat with Guido, who is always working at the international package window. He confesses that it's the best place to meet all the foreign women in Modena. He then digs out another package that he just mailed to Minneapolis to see if I know the person. Of course I don't, but it's a good conversation starter.

I ask him if all the rumors I hear are true that postal employees go through the mail for goodies. "Non è vero! It's not true!" he replies indignantly. "We don't search through the mail!" Then he thinks a minute and whispers, "Well, we did catch one of my colleagues with a whole library of videocassettes, CDs, and books, but that's unusual. I think he even got fired, which in Italy is very difficult to do!"

I show him an article I clipped from the newspaper about a post office in Rome that was robbed by a contortionist midget. The thief mailed himself to the post office and then burglarized it at night. Guido's reaction is the same as many people's: he's impressed by the imagination of the daring crook.

He tells me in Naples people are even more creative. Some guys make a cash machine. Someone hides inside the cash machine as people put their card in and punch their secret number. The thief inside carefully writes down the PIN and holds onto the cash card. Once the customer walks away to complain that the card has been stolen, the man comes out of the ATM and uses the card at a different machine. "Now that's creative!" Guido says.

I tease Guido that I'm a little worried my nephew won't get his gift. I'd better not catch him walking around Modena with a frog umbrella.

A couple of weeks later, I stop in the post office to talk to Guido, and the renovation is completed after more than two years of work. The atmosphere is now industrial and cold with polished marble floors, brass fixtures, fresh cement, and lots of glass. The only windows to the outside have iron bars on them. All the postal employees seem happy to work in this "improved" building. Customers, on the other hand, can't hear a word the workers are saying, so we have to shout a couple of inches from the glass to be heard. The marble room serves as an echo chamber, so I only hear vague shouting. Since the glass isn't bulletproof and just serves as a separator, I suggest Guido put a small hole in the glass. Guido's colleagues say that would ruin the new look of the building and the customers will just have to live with the new system.

Since I can't talk to Guido at the post office anymore, we arrange to meet for a *passeggiata* around the center of town. As I'm walking to meet him, a little Italian lady blocks the sidewalk and orders me, "Giovanotto! Young man! Come here!" She points to her 50cc three-wheeler car, which older people drive when they have their driver's license taken away. These little glorified covered scooters are far more dangerous than actual automobiles, but no license is needed, so teenagers and elderly drivers clog the streets with them, driving dangerously slow.

"Could you give me a push?" she asks—as if I have a choice. She hops in her little two-stroke automobile, and I begin huffing and puffing behind her down the street. "Faster, faster," she yells as I'm struggling with my book bag over my shoulder and everyone on the sidewalk watching the scene. After a few blocks, I'm dripping with sweat as she steps out and tells me I can go. "This damn car hasn't been working for weeks!" she adds.

I finally meet Guido on Via Emilia, and he's standing in front of the post office chatting with his coworkers. Little by little, I realize Guido is an unlikely Casanova. He's traveled all over Europe visiting his girlfriends, but he doesn't strike me as some super-slick Italian stallion with Armani suits and a cigarette dangling from his lips. He never hides behind sunglasses or brags. Instead, he wears his pants a little too high and has an old red Fiat Panda (the "Dance" model), a disarming smile, and a weakness for buffalo milk mozzarella, something to which I can relate. In other words, the kind of guy with whom women feel at ease.

He says whenever he meets an American woman, they almost always tell him, "I can't believe your name is really 'Guido.' Do you know what connotations that has in English?" He has to act surprised and interested. "Oh really? In Italian it means 'I drive.'"

Guido dates mostly foreign women. Over the course of the next couple of months, I meet a few of his multinational force. He seems to be in a rut since all of their names begin with a letter that doesn't exist in Italian: J. There's Janice, Janka, Judit, Judith, Juko. Or perhaps he's just working his way through the alphabet.

He readily admits he's confused about the mentality of

Italian women. "Italian women *have to* have a boyfriend, otherwise who do they go out with on Saturday night? If things don't work out with their steady boyfriend, they'll always have a backup."

The idea of a "date" seems foreign to them since Italians always want to go out in big groups for pizza or to a pub. The women almost never order anything more than fruit juice or a very small beer to drink. This doesn't stop men, however, from asking if women want another. My shoe salesman student, Davide, explains the expression *Non si può avere la botte piena e la moglie ubriaca,* which means "You can't have your cake and eat it too" but is literally "You can't have your barrel of wine full and a drunk wife too"—the two best things in life, apparently.

Getting drunk is frowned upon by Italians because it's considered making a *brutta figura.* Driving after downing a bottle of wine at the *enoteca* is common since drivers will insist they're perfectly in control. Questioning driving ability is tantamount to asking for a fight. Putting on a seat belt begs the question "Are you afraid?" or still worse "Don't you trust me?" Unfortunately, Sunday newspapers have "Le Strage di Sabato Sera" (The carnage of Saturday night after drinking at the discotheque) splashed across the front page with gruesome photos.

Guido explains that the rules about dating in Modena are different from in Naples, his hometown. "Wednesday night is with the amorosa [girlfriend or boyfriend], Friday night is with friends, Saturday night with the amorosa, and Sunday is spent with the family. Couples date for years and years, and sometimes the woman remains a virgin that whole time. After ten or fifteen years, they make wedding plans, look for a house, then break up a week before the wedding. It happens all the time."

While we're walking around, Guido's cell phone rings, and his face lights up, "Ciao mamma!" He must go shopping because his mom wants him to bring a kilo of Parmigiano-Reggiano when he goes home to Naples over the weekend. I suppose he's sort of a cheese broker because he promises me he'll bring some fresh mozzarella back north to Modena.

On Saturday night, Katy and I stop by our neighborhood pizzeria, and the young Neapolitan *pizzaiolo* (pizza maker), Salvatore, decides to confide his life story to us. I'm surprised to find how important it is for southern Italian men that their *amorosa* be a virgin. "It's important that I was the first with her," he tells us. "Then I escaped. Now her parents want us to get married. Her father wants me to return to work in his tobacconist shop. I just can't do it. Then there's the problem of her best friend. I got her pregnant, and now my uncle is taking care of her in an apartment in Genoa. My girlfriend doesn't know about her best friend and me, and she doesn't know where I am either."

Just then, the ringing telephone interrupts his story. "How did you find my number?" he shouts into the receiver. "Don't call here again! I'll call you!" He hangs up the phone and says, "That was my girlfriend. I don't know how she found my number at the pizzeria. I love her very much but do not want to live with her and work in her father's tobacconist shop."

It seems that couples rarely live together before they're married; if they do, they're considered married. It's perfectly normal to live at home with one's parents until at least thirty-five years old. This way, rent's free, food's good, and clothes are perfectly ironed. In fact, I'm sure this supports the Italian fashion industry because these young people have money to blow on the latest shoes. Supposedly, these stay-at-home twenty- to thirty-year-olds spend about half their income on clothes.

On Monday morning, the English teacher from Manchester comes into the Lord Arnold School scraped up after he hung one on the night before. "The last thing I remember is that I fell off a wall." While he laughs at the stupidity of the situation, the Italians in the school are horrified and say they would never admit to something like that.

The idea of being seen as an out-of-control drunk is horrifying to Italians, but this reaction seems strangely puritanical when I think about a musician friend from Modena who brags about all the prostitutes he's bedded. Whenever he drives me to his studio to play some of his new music, he finds an excuse to drive by the huge queue of African *puttane,* as he calls them, wearing nearly nonexistent miniskirts, lined up next to the family shopping mall. When parents bring their kids to the COOP shopping center, they have to drive down the gauntlet of truck drivers propositioning prostitutes. When I ask my musician friend if his girlfriend knows about his liaisons and if most Italian men are like this, he replies, "No, no. Of course not. Some men are faithful, otherwise women would never believe any men. These are the men, the saints, who make everything possible for the rest of us."

Somehow, couples usually stay together in spite of this mentality. Another teacher tells me that she took a class in Italy, and the female chaperone asked the young women students what they would do if they caught their boyfriend cheating on them. All the foreigners responded they'd dump him immediately. A young Italian woman then piped up, "I'd be angry at first, but I would take him back." While the foreign students were shocked, the teacher looked at her satisfied and said, "Brava, brava."

For me, this battle of the sexes makes a perfect discussion topic for my English lessons to get the students to speak. My students can't believe that in Vegas couples can get married one night and divorced the next, all for just $99! They tell me that in Italy divorce now takes only three years.

After one of our lessons, a student who is an attorney hands me her card and says, "If you know anyone who needs a lawyer, just tell me. You know, to get married or . . . " She pauses, then whispers excitedly, "or even divorced. I know it's terrible, but it does happen!"

While the Vatican has pushed to keep divorce illegal in Italy, a national vote on a referendum overwhelmingly made it legal. Likewise, the Pope lost his battle against banning birth control, sex education, and premarital sex in Italy. Even so, newspapers still carry stories like the one of the thirteen-year-old who thought she had bad gas. She went to the bathroom and gave birth.

The birthrate in Italy is now negative because people are getting married later and later. Having children is so expensive now, and many younger people want to enjoy themselves rather than be stuck at home with kids like their parents were. When a child is born, the relatives dote on the new little royalty. Being in Italy, I don't feel so bad about not getting married at the ripe young age that my parents did.

After class one day, Guido calls to tell us he's back from Naples. "You must come over to my apartment to eat the mozzarella from la mamma," Guido tells me. "If I eat it all, I will be huge! It will be no good tomorrow, so we must finish it now!" I never say "no" to fresh mozzarella: my favorite food.

I tease Guido that he's a *mammone,* or mama's boy, but by Italian standards, he's far from it. He has his own apartment and is completely self-sufficient, although he doesn't mind when his mother visits and spends her entire time cleaning.

Guido says his favorite food isn't mozzarella but the chocolate-hazelnut spread Nutella. I ask if I can taste some of it, but his usual generous nature turns stingy. "Sorry. Perhaps I'm more Genovese than Napoletano," making reference to the reputation of miserly people from Genoa. "I never share my Nutella. It's like underwear; there are certain things you don't share with friends."

After the mozzarella-eating spree, we take a stroll through the piazza to catch up. I notice all the public posters announcing weddings. Apparently, couples have to announce their nuptials at least two weeks ahead of time in public, in case one of them is already married.

We see a fancy wedding party pour out onto the steps of a church. Katy says, "That is so romantic," as she sees the beautiful young bride step out of the medieval church. The crowd is waiting anxiously for the groom to step out of the church. "Oh my goodness," Katy says, aghast, and covers her mouth. The graying groom is easily old enough to be the bride's father and walks carefully down the steps to avoid slipping.

I ask Guido if this is typical. He tells us a joke that he says sums up the mentality of the Mediterranean male—at least those from southern Italy. "A Neapolitan guy is deserted on an island with supermodel Claudia Schiffer, who falls madly in love with him. Boom, bang, all day long! One day, he's very depressed, and she asks him what's wrong. 'I miss all my friends back home in Naples. Do you think you could put on a beard and pretend you're one of my friends?' 'I guess so, if it will make you happy,' she replies. So Claudia Schiffer puts on a beard and then taps him on the shoulder. He turns around and says, 'Gaetano! Ciao! You'll never guess what I just did. I made it with Claudia Schiffer!'"

According to Guido, "Many Italian guys think the girl-friend is just for show, and that's why you meet your buddies in the piazza!" Which would explain why many Italian men marry women ten or more years younger even though they may have little in common.

While Guido understands this mentality, he seems to prefer the chase. He has recently joined a Buddhist group because of some prospects. He shows me all the chants he had to read to achieve his desires.

That exploit came to an end, and now Guido is saving up for a big trip to visit his new girlfriend in Scandinavia. It's February, so I ask if he's ever experienced true winter. "They told me the weather is great right now, but I'm bringing sweaters and my big coat anyway." We look up Sweden's weather in the *Herald Tribune* and find a low of nineteen and high of thirty. "See! It's already spring there!" I tell him this is Fahrenheit. When we do the conversion into Celsius, Guido's face goes pale. "Why would anyone live there?"

Guido is also worried his new squeeze will accidentally discover all his e-mail messages from other women when he's on her computer in Sweden. "At first, all you had to do was be sure you didn't call her by a different name. Now you have to make sure she doesn't read your e-mail and listen to your phone messages!"

Arrangiati!

The *Corriere della Sera* newspaper recently announced that the government in Rome is proud that Italy has only about thirty thousand laws. Opposition politicians estimate there are more like one hundred thousand, but no one's quite sure, which seems a bit worrisome. Either way, Italy has more laws than probably any other country, but most are rarely enforced.

For example, if a new tax law is passed, some Italians will hold their breath and hope the law or prime minister is soon changed. New laws sometimes make the old laws illegal, which makes obeying the law in the first place a risky proposition. In general, it's best to wait it out. New elections can't be too far away.

The verb *arrangiarsi*—literally meaning "to arrange yourself" but more accurately "to work the system"—sums up the Italian knack of surviving in spite of a generally unfriendly government. When many Italians immigrated to the United States and brought this well-practiced survival tactic, some got the reputation of being corrupt.

When I try to obey all the laws in Italy, I realize I'm being naive. To renew our *permesso di soggiorno*, "permission to stay," for another three months, we cross the border into Slovenia to get a new, automatic tourist visa. The guard, however, lets me right back into Italy without restamping my passport. I ask him if he can stamp my passport, thereby validating me for another three-month stay. He becomes suspicious and hauls me aside for questioning. When I tell him I wrote a book about scooters, he warms up and talks to me about his father's 1957 Lambretta for fifteen minutes while my friends are waiting impatiently. He finally stamps my passport but only on the condition that I call him up to shoot a photo of his dad's scooter if I write another book.

Once back in Modena, Katy and I assemble our documents to apply for another *permesso di soggiorno* at the police department, or *questura*. I am finally beginning to understand the language and the bureaucracy. We carry the necessary materials—two photographs, a photocopy of my passport, a letter from the people supposedly hosting us (that our friend Marina wrote), and ten Euros worth of *marca da bollo*, or official government stamps. Most importantly, I've met one of the head people in the *questura*, named Lida, who told me to come see her if I ever need help with my *permesso di soggiorno*.

On the steps of the *questura*, I ask the guard if Lida is in, but he just laughs, "Yeah right, you're friends with Lida. That's what everyone says." He taps the barrel of his submachine gun and indicates for us to get in line like everyone else. I then remember that Guido introduced me to a friend of his, Seba, who works there. I ask the guard if Seba is working. This time the guard doesn't laugh but starts interrogating me about this "friend" to see how well I know him. "What kind of car does he drive?"

"What kind of car?" I respond. "I have no idea."

"Well, what days does he work?" he asks.

"Umm, I don't know his schedule," I respond.

"I can tell that you are not friends then," he says, convinced, and motions with his machine gun for us to get in the long line with everyone else.

When we finally get into the office, Seba comes out from behind his desk and gives us kisses on both cheeks. While other people are waiting impatiently, he asks how life is treating us in Modena.

Once inside the large hallways of the *questura,* I see my friend Lida, who invites us up for a coffee. She says I have to be more insistent with the guard to be let in, but I tell her I'm a little hesitant of being pushy around guys with machine guns. In her office, Lida pulls out the appropriate documents and winks at us knowingly, "You're not 'working' here in Modena, are you?" I was always taught lying to a cop is not a good idea—much less to one of the heads of the police department—nevertheless, I take the cue. I've learned the finer points of how to *arrangiarsi* and assure her that we're not "working." Our *permesso di soggiorno* is immediately approved.

At the Lord Arnold School, I make another friend at the *questura,* a twenty-eight-year-old police captain from Rome. He comes to the school for private English lessons knowing full well that I'm illegal and shouldn't be working. He doesn't care as long as I teach good lessons. He enters the classroom, plops his cell phone and huge pistol on the table with a clunk, and says politely, "I hope you don't mind that I put my gun there; it's just too heavy on my belt."

As we go through verb charts in my English grammar book, I'm careful not to bump his handgun. I can't tell if the safety is set and feel that it's aimed toward me, or that a ricochet off the cement walls would nail me. The lessons inevitably digress to talking about Rome since he doesn't like being stuck in the cold fog of Modena. He nearly gets teary eyed with homesickness. "Just walking around Piazza

Navona and Trastevere in the evening, it's so beautiful. The light, the air, the gelato . . . there's magic in Rome."

My heart skips a beat when his vibrating cell phone goes off and shakes the whole table. The vibration moves the pistol as if we're playing spin the bottle or Russian roulette with the barrel aimed ever nearer my heart. "Excuse me, but I need to answer this since I'm on call," he tells me, wiping away tears. Then he reverts to his role as a police captain and yells into his cell phone. He grabs the pistol handle as he screams at his subordinates, and the more he shouts, the tighter he grips his pistol. He slams down the phone, complaining about Albanians and violent soccer fans. He needs to interrupt his lesson to go halt some skirmish at the stadium. He clips his pistol back in the holster, puts his hand on my shoulder, and says affectionately, "If you have any problems, any problems at all, come to me and I'll take care of them for you."

A Risky Subject

The Italian word *argomento* doesn't mean "argument," but it might as well. When I hear a discussion of an *argomento,* or subject, it sounds like an argument to my ears, at least it did until I had a real fight, or *lite* (pronounced LEE-tay). You haven't lived until you've argued in Italian, especially when you know you're right and have nothing to lose. My Italian is hardly up to winning a difficult argument, but I find it easier when I know I have a good case.

The Lord Arnold School is being audited by the Guardia di Finanza, the Italian version of the IRS but more like a SWAT team of tax accountants that swoops down on a business and freezes all work until their scrutiny is done. The management at the school is terrified of being audited, or I imagine so because many businesses cook the books in Italy with one official ledger to show the government and another, more accurate one kept in a very safe spot.

Rumors are flying that the boss, Signor Truffino, will have to go to jail. The secretaries are at once nervous at the prospect of losing their jobs if the school goes belly-up but are also a bit pleased that he might get his comeuppance. We learn, however, that he didn't get to be a knight by being foolish. He's been so sly and *furbo* that the tax inspectors can't quite piece together how much the Lord Arnold School actually owes the government.

The Guardia di Finanza could close down the school and press charges against Signor Truffino, but the taxmen aren't sure what that would solve. Instead, the boss gets off the hook by paying huge fines and has to sell his house to get out of debt. No one at the school dares ask him about it, so rumors are flying about the impact on his family.

He now proclaims the school will go legit this year by forcing contracts on all the teachers. Since most of us don't come from the European Union, we can't sign contracts in Italy without work permits. Employing only properly documented teachers would essentially halve the number of classes the school can offer. Rather than dealing with the mounds of bureaucracy and cost to get each teacher a legitimate working visa, the school declares it will simply assume we're all legal. If the immigration police storm the school, which is highly unlikely, the school will plead innocent, and the burden of proof will be put on us.

The more immediate problem for us teachers, however, is that the school is cutting our wages by 30 percent so they can pay our income tax. They haven't paid any Italian income tax up to this point, and many of the teachers are skeptical this 30 percent will actually be given to the state. As part of going legit, Signor Truffino refuses to pay us for our previous work until we sign this annual contract forcing us to work the whole new year at about $8 an hour.

I know I have to quit Lord Arnold and just give private lessons, but luckily I have already borrowed from the boss as much money as he owes me from working the past month. I've learned well from Signor Truffino's not paying the past three months' rent on some of his apartments: Never let the other party hold all the cards.

My first reaction is to not bother going back to the school to speak with Signor Truffino and to just call it even. Instead,

I figure this is a great learning opportunity for my Italian. Guido gives me some advice and some new vocabulary such as *bustarella* (bribe) and *ricatto* (blackmail) to use when I meet the boss.

I naively pronounce to Signor Truffino that we should negotiate our contract after we've been paid for work completed so it isn't like a *ricatto*. It's hard to know how powerful a word can be in another language, but as I watch my boss's face turn pale then red with fury, I realize I've stepped over the line. He proclaims, "Ricatto? How dare you say I'm blackmailing you!" He shouts all sorts of insults at me, which I busily look up in my pocket-sized dictionary.

Against my better judgment, I follow Guido's advice and toss out more inflammatory words, such as *imbroglione* (swindler) and *ladro* (thief). Amazingly enough, these insults calm the boss down. Perhaps we both needed to get our thoughts out on the table.

I have no intention of continuing to work for the school, but Signor Truffino offers me a deal as long as I promise not to tell the other teachers. He scribbles little graphs he thinks will convince me to stay. "Work, work, work! Money, money, money!" is written underneath the chart. He assures me the 30 percent taken out of my paycheck will be paid to the Italian government as taxes, but then the U.S. government will reimburse me this money. I've heard of this mutual income tax system with the United States, but my taxman in Minnesota says the application process is nearly impossible. I'm surprised my boss expects me to trust the Italian bureaucracy to work in my favor, especially when he's still trying to evade it. Besides, both Signor Truffino and I know I don't have a work visa, so if I file for this money in the United States, both of us could be in trouble.

The boss then throws away that graph and comes up

with a new system to pay my old salary without the 30 percent cut. Part of the payment will be on the books, and the
rest will be under the table. I must provide stacks of receipts
so he can have some evidence if the Guardia di Finanza find
out about me. While he thinks he's making a concession, I
sense a strange satisfaction because he's proved that he's
indeed corrupt. Besides, he adds, if I don't accept his terms,
he'll sue me for not completing my "virtual contract." If that
doesn't work, I'm sure he'd consider turning me in for working in Italy illegally. Although if he notified the authorities
about my work in Italy, it would just bring the Guardia di
Finanza back to his door. The situation is very confusing,
but we both have something on each other.

Rather than getting in any deeper, I take Guido's advice
and just murmur the word *ricatto* again and walk out. The
boss is furious and hurls insults at me. As I'm leaving the
building, Signor Truffino yells, "All your colleagues are
laughing at you! They all think you're a fool!" A couple of the
secretaries secretly give me the thumbs-up sign. Even though
I'm out of a job, I have no regrets except that I hadn't con-
cealed a tape recorder in my jacket to record the conversation for my friends and the Guardia di Finanza in case they
come after me. In any case, I know people in the *questura*
who could help me out.

In a couple of days, I receive a threatening letter from
the boss saying that he's very disappointed by my behavior.
Signor Truffino claims he's going to send letters to people in
Minnesota warning them about me. When I phone one of
the secretaries to ask if he's serious, she just laughs and says
it's his standard letter to employees who quit to make them
nervous.

I show the letter to my friends at the *questura* to see if I
need to be worried. They tell me that I should file a *denuncia*,

denouncing him, even though it's illegal for me to be working in Italy. This sounds like adding fuel to the fire, so I resist. Besides, it would probably just be lost on the stack of other *denunce,* like the one for my stolen bike.

I've overheard conversations before as to how handy the *denuncia* can be in Italy. A student of a friend worked at a clothing shop in Modena but was tired of her boss's denying her a raise, hiding profits, and other shenanigans. She knew he was cooking the books, so she denounced him anonymously to the *questura.* Then she quit her job. She couldn't find another job, so she ended up getting hired back at the clothing store because her boss never knew who denounced him. Perhaps the police are pros at keeping secrets and using the witness protection programs with all of the Mafia *denunce.*

In my case, however, I'm sure my boss, Signor Truffino, would have a pretty good idea of the culprit, so I leave the ball in my old boss's court.

For more advice, I show the letter to my friend Antonio, who has a mysterious knack for knowing all the intricacies of Italian bureaucracy. Antonio looks at the letter in disbelief and laughs, "Look! He called you a 'soggetto rischioso' [risky subject]! It's really quite an honor. Did you know the official definition of a 'risky subject' is a person listed as a truly dangerous crook by Interpol in Brussels? He must consider you a very important criminal." Perhaps my dream of joining an international espionage ring will be realized after all.

In any case, I have to admit I am worried to have as my new archenemy someone who has officially been dubbed a *cavaliere,* or knight, according to the award on his wall. That night, I dream of the carvings on Modena's cathedral of King Arthur and his noble knights teamed up with Lord Arnold. I'm the ne'er-do-well imposter and no match for these proud paladins.

While worrying about my fate, I hear about a British teacher who has a much bigger argument with the boss a week later that nearly comes to blows. The letters denouncing me to the governor of Minnesota, the president of the United States, and anyone else the boss can think of have probably been forgotten.

I also hear the liaison with the Ukrainian secretary has come to a head. The boss's wife finally had solid evidence of the affair and confronted the pair during a meeting of the secretaries. The Ukrainian secretary yelled back at the wife, "You can have him! I'm sick of him! He's a pain in the neck!"

Strangely, I begin to feel sorry for Signor Truffino because he did give me a job (for which I was partially paid) and taught me by example how to be truly *furbo*.

I hear that the situation improved for him after these last battles. The Ukrainian and the boss's wife have buried the hatchet and become great friends. Now that the Ukrainian woman needs a place to stay, the wife lets her stay at their house. I can't imagine what an uncomfortable situation this must be. Rumor has it the affair is continuing, however, and the Ukrainian woman is using her situation to bargain for a paid trip to the UK. The wife happily convinces the husband to bankroll the extended stay in Britain for the Ukrainian.

A few weeks afterward, one of the secretaries calls to tell me I need to come sign a *Modulo 101*, even though I don't work for the school anymore. "It's really nothing," she assures me, "just another document, and we need your signature."

Out of curiosity, I stop by the school to see what on earth this could be. Signor Truffino is away on a trip to Ukraine supposedly on business, so a new tax accountant shows me the *Modulo 101*, a tax form for money I was supposedly paid by the school. Apparently, the Guardia di Finanza have continued their audit, so the school is trying to get their books in order. When I explain that I was never paid, the accountant is surprised because someone received the money. She wants me to sign because "it's all just bureaucracy anyway and won't make any difference." I tell her I'd rather not, and I say, "addio" (good-bye). Even if the boss fakes my signature, at least I'm not complicit.

On the way out, one of the secretaries stops me, very upset. She doesn't think I should leave my classes without a teacher. Even though she knows the boss doesn't want to pay me without my signing a questionable contract, she feels I owe it to my students to stay. I explain my financial situation: the boss owes me a month's salary, but I've borrowed money from him for the damage deposit on our apartment. I tell her that I regret not being able to just call it even with him because he's been nice in lending me the money and leasing his apartments to other foreign teachers.

"Oh, don't worry about that," she replies. "The boss always charges tenants extra on the rent so he can pay for the apartment when it's empty. If he rents it all year-round, he makes a big profit from those teachers." Suddenly, I feel a little less remorse.

Casino or Casinò?

Working as a journalist in Italy isn't done for the pay, but for the perks. My editor, Roberto, orders me to come to the newspaper office right away—it's always right away—for a very important and lucrative assignment.

Journalists are the same the world over. They smoke too much because of the stress of their deadlines and never have a moment to talk—except to say how stressed out they are because of deadlines and that they shouldn't smoke so much.

Roberto has three telephones: one land line, a personal cell phone (or *telefonino*), and an office cell phone. Often he's on all three phones at the same time, and someone is always put on hold. While I wait in person, he occasionally covers the receiver and tells me, "Non ne posso più!" (I can't stand it anymore!).

Today, though, he has a new toy, a teddy bear that dances and sings in the Neapolitan dialect. "Bellissimo!" Roberto raves. "È la cosa più bella che abbia mai visto in vita mia!" (It's the most beautiful thing I've ever seen in my life!). Before he can tell me about my new assignment, I simply must agree with him on the beauty of his toy.

After we listen to all the bear's songs, a Moroccan man comes into the office to sell him a pair of socks. Roberto doesn't brush him off, as so many people do, but is polite with him—at first. Roberto says, "You sold me a pair last week, and they made my feet sweat so badly my wife won't come near me." The Arab views this as an opportunity to sell him a higher-quality (and more expensive) pair of socks, but Roberto tells him to please leave him alone saying, "What are you trying to do, break up my marriage?"

While he's arguing to be left in peace, I pick up the latest edition of our weekly newspaper of Modena. On the front cover is an Italian case of sexual harassment in which the judge ruled a little pat on the butt is OK, but touching breasts isn't. A huge close-up photo of bulging breasts has a big "NO!!" written across them; next to it is a woman's butt with her underwear going up her crack that says "Sì??" This is the weekly newspaper that carries my column.

Roberto breaks off negotiations with the Moroccan sock salesman, but he has a fresh pair of polyester beauties. He turns to me, "What are you waiting for? Get going!" He says I must go home right this instant and pack my bags since we're leaving for Slovenia tomorrow morning on a junket. He will pick me up at 5 a.m., and a representative of a Slovenian casino will drive us to their entertainment complex for the night; I have to write an article about our stay.

I don't know how Roberto arranged this new adventure, but I agree since the other assignments we've gone on have been thoroughly amusing. A month ago, he sneaked me into a big dinner with hundreds of farmers who were celebrating an anniversary of Landini tractors. Roberto handed me the microphone to give an impromptu speech—simply because I'm American. It made no difference that I know nothing about tractors; the farmers told me they were honored to have me there and presented me with a special award.

Now, we're in the car for the three-hour car trip to Nova Gorica, Slovenia. I imagine I'll have lots of time to chat with

Roberto, but he's on his cell phone most of the time because of inevitable crises at the newspaper.

We venture through the killing fields south of Udine, foggy plains where thousands of Italian soldiers died in World War II. At the border crossing, lines of Fiats are waiting to take advantage of the undervalued Eastern European currency. The Slovenian government is doing everything it can to attract Italian tourists over the border to visit its casinos. Digital announcement boards attached to the top of the customs officers' house advertise, "Table Dance! Lesbo Show! Hot babes under the shower!" Because of the limitations of the digital sign, the address is written without an accent over the letter *o* in *casinò*, which unintentionally changes the meaning of the word in Italian from "gambling casino" to "whorehouse."

Our fancy four-star hotel complex sits below a beautiful hilltop monastery. I ask the receptionist about the ancient church, and she tells me, "Oh, it's just some old building that takes a long time to get to. There's much more happening at the casino. You never need to leave!"

We don't take her advice and instead go for a *passeggiata*. We don't venture up to the monastery, but we admire a huge monument outside the hotel dedicated to Communist heroes who liberated Yugoslavia from the capitalists. In the center of town, a tent has been set up to sell fresh wine. Although it looks tempting, a few young thugs have had a few too many and hurl insults at us "Italians" as we walk away. I realize now why the receptionist recommends never leaving the casino/hotel/restaurant/fortress.

Just then, busloads of Italians storm the casino, mostly from Modena. I try in vain to interview them for the article. They have no time to chat and nearly bowl me over to get to the slot machines. A fight breaks out between a couple of older women over a one-arm bandit that is "hot." The management quickly breaks up the battle; apparently this is a common occurrence.

Roberto's unhappy with our room, even though it's absolutely free, so he calls down to request plush bathrobes. "It's the least they can do," he tells me. We stop down at the pool for a dip before dinner, and I convince Roberto to come to the fancy sauna. We're both a little shocked that everyone is nude. I wonder if this is what the advertisements could have meant by "Hot babes under the shower!" The portly crowd in the sauna doesn't fit the description, so we follow suit to blend in with the locals.

The management tells me dinner is "free-flow," which doesn't sound particularly appetizing, but they mean it's an all-you-can-eat buffet. This concept is unusual in Europe, and once-cordial people elbow and eat like it's their last meal. In Slovenia, they want their casino to be like "American" ones, whereas in Las Vegas they aim for the Italian ideal with Caesar's Palace and a replica of Venetian canals.

I ask a representative from the casino who sits down to eat with us if she thinks it's odd the government owns this casino and maybe locals will lose any money they have on the slots. She tells me with certitude worthy of Communist-era tour guides, "We Slovenians don't gamble, so it's not a problem." She adds that many people come just for dinner and entertainment, "It's a family atmosphere." Just then, the evening show starts with topless women and men dancing high-kicking choreographed routines with peacock feathers. More people are interested in the soccer game as team Italia is playing Belgium tonight. At the end of the game a few fans interrupt the dance screaming, "Merda!" Even Italy is losing tonight.

As we check out the next morning, Roberto is once again

unhappy with how we're being treated when the reception-ist asks us to pay for the drinks we took from the minibar. To avoid a scene, I pay for the overpriced drinks. Once out the door, Roberto tells me he got even with the hotel since he stuffed the plush bathrobes into his bag and will give me one when we return to Modena.

A couple of weeks after our adventure to Slovenia and the subsequent story I wrote, I stop by the newspaper to pick up my payment for the article. Roberto is busy download-ing music from the Internet on his fancy new computer as his wife is waiting to go out to lunch with him. "Keep on Rockin' in the Free World" is blasting as he tells me they called from the casino asking to be reimbursed for the bath-robes. He was incensed they would accuse him of stealing after they treated us so poorly. The casino apologized for the confusion.

I remind him that we did steal the bathrobes. His wife says, "I don't know why he wants another bathrobe any-way! He already has three of them at home." Roberto shakes his head and insists it's the principle of the matter.

Commie Pigs?

I think my friend Antonio is a spy. He seems a little too obvious, though. He claims he works for a publicity company, yet he jet sets off to NATO conferences in Brussels and Geneva. He explains how he avoids getting locked up or questioned during his "vacations" in Moscow. He gives long, academic speeches on local TV every week but wrote a book called *Europe Is a Sow*. In fact, he often speaks about the pigs, by which I assume he means the Communists in Modena.

Perhaps Antonio is an eccentric millionaire who drives an old white Fiat Uno, which he jokes is the same kind of car a gang of bad policemen used to terrorize the country until a sixteen-year-old Romanian prostitute turned them in.

He tells me loyalties in Modena depend on who is in power. Everyone was proud to be a Fascist during the war; then they were all partisan Communists when the tide turned. Enzo Ferrari might have been soft on the Fascists but was probably sneaking money to the partisans just in case. Any good businessman gave money to both sides. Is Antonio telling me to play nationalities off each other like a good double agent?

He found out about me through the U.S. consulate in Florence while he was allegedly looking for an American to help translate for one of his projects. We've been living in Italy illegally—technically speaking—and lying low to avoid being suddenly deported, but somehow the U.S. government knew all about me living in Modena. I'm spooked that the United States keeps tabs on me, even though I never filed any documents with my government telling where I'm living. Perhaps the American government taps into the *permesso di soggiorno* papers that I had to file with the Italian *questura*. How Antonio has access to this information, I don't know. Meanwhile, the Italian government knows nothing about me. Or more likely, all the information they have on me is stored safely away under stacks of paper in a bureaucrat's office.

Giving into my fascination with international spy rings, I accept his invitation to an important meeting one evening, by invitation only, of course. He tells me to dress well since many distinguished people will be there. I hope all these VIPs will deem me worthy and inaugurate me into the underground world of espionage.

Antonio tells me one of his colleagues will be presenting a new manual called "Once Upon a Time There Was a Pig." I had no idea there is still so much animosity, with the cold war being over for years. Only two hundred copies have been printed and distributed to a select group. Most of those who received this instructional booklet will be in attendance; the rest are incognito in undisclosed locations.

The group of Italian men in stiff gray suits cordially greet each other; then Antonio takes the stage. "We are gathered here this evening, as we all know, to talk about pigs," he announces. As the members of the audience munch on prosciutto and sausage pizza washed down with bubbly Lambrusco, I translate the sign behind the podium as "Italian Association of Salami Tasters." I can't figure out any irony or code words. Rather than being in the midst of 007s, I'm surrounded by pork producers.

Between bites of pork, the hefty man next to me mumbles, "Antonio has one of the largest collection of pig figurines in the world!" I figure that even the CIA wouldn't use someone so silly as a front for a spy.

Antonio turns over the microphone to the evening's special guest, an author of a new book on pigs. "The work of putting together this book was done, of course, only out of passion," the author confesses. "After all, this is an infinite subject.

"In Milan, they presented a book on pigs, but what was it? Only recipes! In my book, however, I reveal when the first time the word *pork* was shown, in a Spanish recipe, and *maiale* (pig) from ancient Latin texts."

The professor/author confesses, "Due to circumstances, I was forced to become a doctor and professor at the University of Pavia and wasn't able to follow my real passion . . . pigs! I soon learned, however, that pigs played an important role in Pavia in the fifteenth century where anatomy classes at the university studied pigs when cadavers were scarce." I wonder if Michelangelo and Leonardo da Vinci drew dead pigs when human corpses were hard to come by.

As the salami producers nod their approval and finish off plates of pork, the author continues. "Pigs were often thought to be medicinal. A medieval remedy for abdominal pain and old age reads, 'burn a pig's heel until the blackened part turns white, then mince it and drink it up.'"

While Antonio serves spicy *coppa* salami, the professor recalls how the little pig of Saint Anthony went to hell. When the devil cracked open the door to show the saint what a horrible place inferno was, the curious piglet wandered in. Anthony disguised himself and ventured into hell to retrieve his companion, but his wooden staff ignited from the flames. This is how fire was brought to humans—all thanks to a pig.

Never Trust a Thin Cook

Si mangia bene, si paga poco! (you eat well, you pay little) is the Italian paradise and the best possible review a restaurant can receive. While making a gesture of filling up a fat stomach, my Italian friends tell me I have to visit Trattoria Ermes. Italians hate to wait in line at restaurants, but this place is so good that it has a crowd out front hoping to find a spot at the five tables inside.

"Never trust a thin cook" is an old Italian proverb, and Signor Ermes is anything but underfed. Ermes's arms are as wide as my waist, and his hands are like flailing meat hooks. He's a potbellied Santa Claus carrying platters of pork. Not to say that he's lazy, by any means. Ermes moves around his tiny restaurant with winged feet like the god for whom he's named.

Almost every morning, I see Ermes riding his black bicycle below my window on Vicolo Forni to the market. Everyone knows him and greets him simply by his first name, Ermes. A few minutes later, he stacks the day's shopping precariously on his bicycle rack and pedals back to the *trattoria*, where his wife cooks up a feast in the tiny kitchen.

The doors open at noon. Ermes doesn't have a phone, so reservations are impossible. If you want to eat there, just show up. He greets us, "Ciao bimbi," (Hi, babies), since to him all people, even little old ladies, are *bimbi*. Ermes scolds me with a big wooden spoon when I arrive. "You know you have to come early! How many times do I have to tell you!"

On the door to his little *trattoria* is a sticker for the "Slow Food" organization of historic *trattorie*, but Ermes doesn't know much about it. When I explain what "slow food" means in English, Ermes sighs and says, "Well, we try to serve the food as fast as possible."

The atmosphere is entertaining but hardly relaxing. You never know when Ermes will ask you to scoot over to make room for more people or sit down himself for a breather. I once brought an overweight American friend to the restaurant, and the regulars were so impressed they yelled, "Dio Buono! Good Lord! He's even bigger than Ermes!" The guest got the place of honor at the head of the table.

To stave off hunger, Ermes immediately brings an antipasto plate of salami and *ciccioli* (essentially all the extra pork parts mashed together with extra fat and pronounced CHEE-choo-lee). There's never a written menu, so he lists all the first courses of the day in a single breath, "For primo piatto, we have tortellini-in-brodo-tortelloni-di-ricotta-con-salvia-o-la-panna-fegatini-ai-quadretti-tagliatelli-al-ragù."

I see that he has *cervello di maiale* sometimes, and I ask if it's really what I think it is. "Oh yes, it's pig's brain. Molto buono!" Memories of eating beef brains in Brescia swirl through my head. Since mad cow disease has hit, brain eaters have deemed pig's brains much cleaner. I wince at the thought, which is the wrong reaction. Ermes insists I taste a little of it.

Today, I'm with Katy—who is notoriously indecisive with menus—so I have to repeat this list to her and explain the details. Ermes shifts impatiently from foot to foot. When she looks up, Ermes's huge fist is inches from her face as if he's going to hit her. He laughs, retracts his fist, and tells us that he'll choose something for us. He scribbles some chicken scratch on his pad of paper and disappears.

Ermes's son asks what we want to drink but then just opens the big cooler and tells us, "Just take what you want. If you need more, help yourself!" Although this fridge has "Coca-Cola" written in huge letters on its side, only bottled water and wine are inside. No wine list exists, since there's only delicious fizzy white or Lambrusco di Sorbara. The sediment in the bottom of the wine just proves it isn't the industrial hooch most people associate with Lambrusco sent stateside.

When a break in the action allows Ermes a few seconds, he's back reading off the second course like a submachine gun, "Guanciale-al-Chianti-lo-zampone-il-bollito-le-costine-alla-cacciatora-scaloppine-all'aceto-balsamico-o-al-limone-coniglio-al-forno-o-bistecca-fiorentina." If you don't understand something, Ermes will indicate the cut of meat simply by pointing to it on his own body.

Woe to those who don't finish everything on their plates! Ermes will be very disappointed and may make you stay there until you're done. If you actually manage to finish and don't need to run to work right away, there's always a card game—usually *briscola* or *scopa*—to be played while trying to empty the fridge of Lambrusco. On the way out the door, I thank the chef, his wife, Bruna. "She's a saint!" one of the satisfied diners yells.

Another customer wonders, "Well, what does that make Ermes then?"

"Hmm, he must be the devil!" the other jokes while ducking from Ermes, who threatens with his wooden spoon.

While paying the bill (it's always a flat fee for everything, including wine), I tell Ermes I want to write an article for the newspaper about his *trattoria*. His son overhears and begs me, "Please don't write good things about the restaurant, because we want *less* people! If you write how good the food is, then you'll have to wait in line longer!"

I stop back at Trattoria Ermes to show him the article a few days after it's published. His arms are full with plates of *tagliatelle*, and without losing a noodle, he manages to nod toward the wall to show me that the article is already framed and signed from all his buddies. Ermes offers me a free meal, and I kick myself for already having eaten a giant meal. I explain that I'm just stopping by to see his son, who mentioned hosting an English class in the neighborhood.

Ermes's son says we shouldn't start the course, since the neighborhood association is about to decide whether to disband because they don't have any classes this year. I suggest if we have a class, the organization would have an excuse to keep together. He rebuts that he doesn't want to make a *brutta figura* and have to cancel the class halfway through the year. I propose we run the course for only half a year but realize I've crossed the line.

Ermes sets down his plates and takes me outside. He affectionately puts his enormous arm around my neck and asks if I'm trying to set up his son to make him a *brutta figura*. Well aware that he could snap my head off by accident, I assure Ermes I have no such intention. The blood to my brain is slowly cut off as he explains that if his son makes a *brutta figura*, it reflects badly on all of us, and we wouldn't want that, would we? I try to shake my head in agreement but am unable to move because of the giant arm holding my neck in place. I manage to squeak a little, "No."

"Va bene, OK," he says, satisfied. "Now, come inside and have some food!" I don't dare refuse and obediently eat some tortellini, the specialty of the day.

Angry Noodles

Friends back home think Katy and I spend all of our time in Italy sitting around drinking large amounts of espresso and eating pizza. Of course, that is my goal, but sooner or later money runs out and reality sets in. "Just as long as you're in Italy, everything must be wonderful, right?" someone actually asked me.

Most people come to Italy on vacation with money to burn, and have a good time. Earning Euros changes everything. I have to rustle up more students to teach, since journalism pays peanuts and leads to dangerous run-ins with portly restaurant owners who always make me eat more than the last time.

I realize I can't afford to work for another school, especially after I hear from one of my fellow teachers who is still working for the Lord Arnold School. My old crazy boss has decided he has overpaid all the teachers since they haven't worked enough hours. Now at the end of the year, he says the teachers owe him money.

I put the word out to my friends that I'm available to teach private lessons or do translations. A fancy Modenese restaurant named "Fini" hires me to translate the labels on some of their frozen noodles they sell in grocery stores, but I explain many of the names of dishes aren't usually changed into English since the Italian sounds more exotic. They tell me to do it anyway or they'll find someone else. I translate *sugo alla puttanesca* into "the whore's sauce," *pollo alla cacciatore* becomes "the chicken hunter" (or equally silly "the hunter's chicken"), *penne all'arrabbiata* changes into "angry noodles," and *spaghetti alla capricciosa* turns into "naughty noodles."

They're thrilled with the speedy translation, but I think teaching is more my specialty. After all, giving lessons is just another excuse for me to learn Italian and Italian culture by asking students questions and forcing them to respond in English. Besides, I can use my students as characters in my book about Italy.

One new pupil is a nutritionist and is constantly interrupted during the lessons by her cell phone. "No, absolutely not," she yells into the little phone. "And don't call back!" She hangs up and tells me one of her patients asked if she could have another piece of pizza. "It happens all the time. They all want to eat more!"

Another student recently quit law school and wants to travel the world as a representative of a ceramics company. I tell him my friend Stefano from Brescia flies first-class around the world selling office chairs. Suddenly, my student cancels his lessons because he has finally been offered a job as a traveling ceramics salesman. Two weeks pass, and he comes back for another class. He has already quit his job. "The first night, I went to Rimini for work," he tells me. "There I was. Alone in the hotel at nine in the evening. No one to eat dinner with. I didn't know anyone in the town. I just sat there and looked at the wall. Che tristezza! It was the worst night of my life. I don't think I ever want to travel for business again."

To show their gratitude, students invite us out to eat, declaring, "We must go eat a pizza! You don't get real pizza in America!" Davide, my best student, who works for a shoe company, shows us photos of his vacation at the sea, but most of the pictures are of a baby pig being roasted on a spit. "You know in Modena, man's best friend is the pig," he says. "When we go on vacation, it's rare we find pork better than in Emilia, but this newborn piglet was particularly delicious."

My adult students have good intentions to learn English but have a hard time studying since they've been out of school for so long. The excuses they devise for not doing their homework or skipping class are always so elaborate and well thought out that I can only admire their creativity.

One student asked me to be especially tough with him. One evening, however, he hadn't written an essay I had assigned. "I didn't have any ironed shirts, and you know my *mamma* lives in the south," he tells me in search of sympathy. When I smirk at the *mammone* (mama's boy), he keeps trying, "From 7 p.m. to 2 a.m., I pressed my clothes. It's an art! If I didn't iron shirts, I would have had to go to work naked!" To him, the idea of wrinkles is blasphemous.

Another student is a burgeoning entrepreneur and doesn't much care for my suggestion of reading a simplified *Huckleberry Finn*. Instead, he brings a copy of *Wall Street Money Machine* because he doesn't want to read this "children's book." Still, he makes fun of his inspirational feel-good guidebook for capitalists on how to score on the stock market. "You Americans," he scoffs, "you always have to mix up your morals and money!"

Parts of the *Wall Street Money Machine* I read out loud to test his comprehension. "Sometimes you have to stay out of the market. Stocks go up and down, set a buying and selling point, and stick to your guns." He scratches his chin and keeps repeating, "Sì è vero, è proprio vero." (Yes, it's true. It's really true.). He changes the subject to tell about a fantastic new business opportunity that I may want to get in on.

The government is considering having public schools allow advertising in their buildings to fund education. "Just think of how much money could be made off this opportunity!"

The lessons wind down when he realizes that although the English language can open doors of opportunity, there are easier ways to earn money. He starts canceling lessons at the last minute and not paying; his excuses leave little room for me to insist on being paid. Today, he has to move his mother's bones. Apparently, bodies aren't buried indefinitely in Italy. The space is rented. Then after a certain amount of time, the bones are usually moved to a smaller space to allow room for more corpses. I'm told that in one plot, often as many as six coffins are stacked on top of each other. Sometimes, the dirt gets too oily from the disintegrated body fat, so sand is added so the bodies will continue to decompose.

My student has to hurry to move the bones since the rent is up and bodies are often moved without relatives even knowing. When *Tutti Santi* (All Saint's Day, November 1) rolls around, everyone goes to the cemetery for a picnic, and some people may not find their loved ones there anymore. One of my students, Antonella Ferrari, is from the famous car-making family, and a relative's bones were "kidnapped" and held for ransom. The family's remains are sacred and must be guarded.

I have no intention of coming between my entrepreneurial student and his mother's bones, so I'm left with little option but to let him off the hook for paying for missed lessons. Perhaps my student actually did learn his lessons well from *Wall Street Money Machine* and remembers that we Americans don't like to mix our morals and money. All I know is that because he isn't paying for canceled lessons, I'm missing out on more pizza and cappuccino.

Walking over Death

Signs of death are all around in Italy. Churches display bones of martyrs and important citizens. Obituary posters line the streets, and a wreath is put on the door of houses where someone has died. Even the Ghirlandina tower supposedly has some saint's bones tucked away in the top of the spire to watch over the town.

While visiting Vignola, a castle town in the hills, we witness an enormous funeral procession of solemn old men with a slightly out-of-tune marching brass band repeating a mournful dirge. The cars stop and the kids turn off their mufflerless *motorini* since obviously someone important has passed on. They march right into the center of town, where the annual Texan festival is under way with bales of hay stacked up next to potted cacti and a band dressed in cowboy hats and bandanas but playing Italian folk songs with American lyrics. Red-faced Italian shopkeepers in hokey Injun outfits want to get their photo taken next to Katy and me because we're the "authentic" Americans—dressed in Italian clothes. The mechanical bull is switched off, and the country band members take off their cowboy hats in respect to the deceased.

The funeral is for a partisan who helped free the town from the Germans. Each city has tales from World War II and bullet holes in the old buildings to prove them. After the procession, an older man at the café asks where I'm from. I tell him I'm visiting from the United States, and he thanks me for liberating Italy from the Nazi scourge. "Thank you," I reply, "but, you know, I really didn't have that much to do with it."

Not only were these towns battlefields, but also scenes of horrible pestilence. A huge stone in the main Piazza Grande of Modena was the site where unclaimed bodies from disease or wars were displayed for the relatives to recognize and bury. My friend Antonio shows me the "plague church" in Modena built for the Madonna as a last-ditch attempt to rid the scourge from ravaging the town. A huge painting in the church shows the village priests and politicians offering a mini version of the town to an indifferent Virgin Mary and baby Jesus while thousands of pockmarked cripples cry in pain.

Outside the plague church, I tell Antonio that church altars in America generally don't have these gruesome scenes of death. He says, "Oh, it's not just the churches. During the fourteenth century, they had to bury the bodies as quickly as possible. Here, we're standing on top of a mass grave site for victims of the plague."

Super Pig Trotter

Although it seems impossible, the Modenese have discovered something heavier than lard, called *zampone*, which loosely translates as "big shank." The rear legs of pigs are packed with salt to make prosciutto. The hams are periodically poked with sharpened horse bones, which are smelled by the experts. The front legs, on the other hand, are shaved, deboned, and stuffed with extra fatty ground pork for zampone.

An American tourist visiting Modena brought home a zampone to his family for Christmas but assumed it was like prosciutto and didn't cook it. He ate the zampone raw and survived to tell the tale.

When I put the first bite of zampone into my mouth, I practically feel my waist expand. The flavor resembles Spam but richer (if that's possible). I tell some Modenese friends about Spam, our famous Minnesotan "Spiced ham," and they are horrified, "Why would you ever put this in a can?" I explain that the pork is liquefied and shot through tubes into little blue tins, and my friends' faces grow pale.

The only possible way to digest zampone is with large amounts of sparkling red Lambrusco. The wine gives you the courage to keep eating more zampone, and the vicious circle continues.

Escaping this pork mania is futile in Modena, so I decide

to embrace it. My editor, Roberto, invites us to the annual pig festival in the town of Castelnuovo Rangone, a few kilometers from Modena. We convince Guido to drive us there in his little Fiat Panda, promising him free pork, Parmigiano, and Lambrusco.

We know we're getting near when the smell of pig penetrates our nostrils. Katy is worried about having to eat heavy pork trotter, but Guido assures her that Castelnuovo has the finest zamponi in all of Italy and probably the world. Her mind is not put at ease.

In the center of Castelnuovo, a pig sculpture has been erected in the town piazza, but many locals are upset that a statue wasn't raised to a "real" hero. The bronze pig has brought fame to the little town, so removing it now is impossible.

In this pig capital of Italy, a Super Zampone is constructed every year, weighing more than a ton. The skin of several pigs is sewn together and stuffed with the chopped pork to look like a giant front pig leg. For four days this gigantic trotter boils in its own juices, and when it's ready, the whole town gathers for a taste, a big taste. This year, Roberto is in charge of the festivities and hands me the megaphone to give a play-by-play account of the bubbling pork. The crowd laughs at what I say, but I realize I'm probably the butt of the joke due to my poor Italian and thick accent. I don't care, though. Instead their applause gives me the courage to interview the crowned King of Zampone. I ask if he has a "Knights of the Super Zampone Round Table," but he looks at me as though to say, "Are you making fun of us?"

As Excalibur was lifted from the waters by the lady of the lake, the two-thousand-pound piece of pork is raised from the steaming water by a gaggle of professionals dressed in white chef's clothes. The excitement of the crowd grows as the Zampone King deems who is worthy enough to cut the first slice. A few years ago, the enormous Luciano Pavarotti lumbered up on the stage to carve the pork and show the world how a steady diet of zampone can expand a man. This year, the king chooses an enormous bleached-blonde woman, who grabs my microphone and sings *liscio* (Italian polka) to the hungry crowd.

While the throng pushes to get a plate of zampone with beans, Parmigiano cheese, and Lambrusco, I'm pulled aside by Roberto to play the guitar and sing some songs about pigs with a fellow American teacher, Mike, and a journalist, Marina. I agreed to play a few songs, never thinking Roberto would actually make us go through with it. With the mayor and other town dignitaries munching their dinners, we perform a few silly ballads about ham. Marina had reworked the lyrics of "Que Sera, Sera" to be about the local baloney: "Mortadella." The crowd sings along to the chorus about eating lard, baloney, and zampone to try to be as fat as Pavarotti someday. Although we hoped to sing incognito, a local TV station films us and will rebroadcast the mini concert. Now we're assured that any friends we have in town will tease us. Luckily, we're rained out after three songs, and we have to unplug the instruments so an electrical shock doesn't zap us. In the meantime, a trained pig named Grunci (pronounced Groon-chee) entertains the crowd by rolling over and standing on his hind legs when a biscuit is waved above him.

My friend Antonio appears out of the blue to tell Katy and me that a national TV station is filming his pig figurine collection on display in the town tower, and they are about to interview him. We wish him well, but a bigger problem has arisen. The Super Zampone has been completely devoured, and not everyone has been fed. The angry and hungry crowd shouts insults at the cooks, who hastily cook some smaller zamponi to appease them and avoid a riot.

Before we all have too much Lambrusco, we escape the pig fest in Guido's little red Fiat, but the fragrance of zampone stays on our clothes for many, many hours.

Reggio's Blockheads and Bologna's Baloney

To greet people in Modena fresh off the train from Bologna, a huge line of graffiti is spray painted on a brick wall, "GRAZIE A DIO NON SONO BOLOGNESE!" (Thank God I'm not from Bologna!).

Town pride runs deep in Italy and has a name, *campanilismo*, or loyalty to your *campanile*, or church bell tower, which is the highest structure in Italian cities and always shows you which way is home. Mostly, this allegiance means boosting your town at the expense of your neighbors. At least since medieval times, Modena and Bologna have resented each other, as shown by a mock heroic poem written in the fourteenth century by a Modenese writer about the *Secchia Rapita*, or stolen bucket. During the heat of battle, Modena captured this booty from the Bolognesi, and now the bucket stands proudly in the Modena city hall under a Plexiglas protector. A decoy is even on display in the Ghirlandina tower nearby to fool any wise guys wishing to retake it.

A few years ago, some university students from Bologna played a prank by sneaking into the city hall and stealing back the bucket. In its place, they left an enormous *mortadella* (baloney), one of the symbols of Bologna. Even though the bucket was eventually returned, people in Modena told me, "It's just not funny; this is a very serious crime." Others saw the humor in substituting the *secchia rapita* bucket with a *mortadella*. Nevertheless, they never balk at the chance to heckle their neighbors in Bologna, "Obviously they don't respect their food. We couldn't imagine leaving a leg of prosciutto for the Bolognesi!"

During the Middle Ages, Modena was the home of the Este dukes, while Bologna was controlled (and looted) by the Popes. Rome also controlled the southern part of the whole region, so it's called "Romagna," whereas the northern part with Modena is called "Emilia," after the Roman road Via Emilia. I ask a friend from the southern part of the region where Emilia ends and Romagna begins. "Well, there's no real border. Once you travel south from Emilia, you'll know you're in Romagna because everything is a little stronger," he tells me. "The wine is stronger, the cheese is stronger, even the pigs are stronger." Bologna is just north of this border, but the enemy nevertheless.

Bologna is much more lively than Modena, with few tourists compared to Florence and Venice and streets full of university students. New graduates wear a noble laurel wreath around their head but often march around drunk in their underwear as a postceremony tradition. Along with receiving their diploma, students are mocked by smutty posters drawn by classmates of their time at school that are plastered around town. After they graduate, they can climb the Asinelli tower. If they dare go to the top before graduation, they risk never getting their degree and spending the rest of their life as a stupid *asino,* or ass, like the name of the tower insinuates.

Via Zamboni is the main street of the university, and as in most of the town, the sidewalks are covered with *portici,* or arcades, to keep off the rain. The bars along this strip stay open late, and an open bar stool is a rarity. Halfway down the road is a little piazza. My Modenese friend Marina tells me, "That's where they sell drugs and bicycles they steal from Modena." I look for my stolen bikes but see only some punks eating hot dogs.

In the center of town, I follow the crowd crossing the busy street against traffic into the main square, Piazza Maggiore. A bum yells at us, "Is everyone such a Communist in this town that you cross when the light is red?"

Today, a protest is under way in the piazza, next to the fountain of a half-naked Neptune surrounded by sirens squirting water from their breasts. The demonstrators are demanding the legalization of marijuana and have made a huge float of a big joint puffing smoke at the crowd.

Students hang out on the steps of the strange half-finished church in the center—the Vatican halted construction when the Pope found out it was going to be bigger than St. Peter's in Rome. Inside, an enormous painting of hell lines the side of the church to scare the devout into being good—a very different scene from the real life outside the church doors.

Although the night life is exhilarating, walking through hordes of people is tiring, and Katy and I are relieved to return to the relative tranquility of Modena. In my bag, I carry a scandalous postcard that I bought at a newspaper kiosk (and possibly the real reason for the town rivalry): a postcard of tortellini claiming these noodles as their own. Marina laughs at the spurious postcard. "Everyone knows that tortellini were created in Modena's suburb, Castelfranco."

I point out the inflammatory caption at the bottom: "Bologna: Culinary Capital of Italy!" She just points out that people from Bologna are quick to boast their importance by claiming these treasures for themselves. "Next thing you know, they'll claim balsamic vinegar as their own!"

Marina explains that Modenesi make fun of people from

Bologna for being *papi*, or little popes, because they were under the Pope's rule for so long. Marina, who is usually an objective journalist, points out that most of the people in the next town over, Reggio Emilia, have a *testa quadrata*, or square head. I wince at her stereotype. "No really, they do!" she insists. "Just look at their heads sometime."

From the outside, with white marble arcades and bicycles zipping through the walking streets, Reggio Emilia seems very similar to Modena. Perhaps Modenesi are envious that even though the area of Modena and part of Bologna were included in the official production area of Parmigiano-Reggiano, only Parma and Reggio get their names on the cheese. Reggio also has a world-famous preschool that revolutionized kindergarten teaching. "We use the same system at our school in Modena, but everyone goes crazy over Reggio," Marina explains jealously.

The next Saturday, Katy and I go sightseeing in Reggio to see the square heads. Perhaps we've been brainwashed or are overly conscious of Marina's description, but we notice that people do have big blockheads on their shoulders. When we stop for a coffee, I ask the barkeep if he's heard of that label for people from Reggio. "You must have heard that in Modena," he responds, unimpressed. "Well, they used to have teste quadrate, except the mice have chewed off the corners."

With this disfigurement in mind, Katy and I visit Reggio's unusual Basilica of Ghiara, with its ceiling adorned with colorful frescoes framed with rococo cherubs and gilded angel statuettes. On the south wing of the church is the Chapel of the Pawn Shop, with a morbid painting by Alfonso Chierici called "Madonna with St. Lucy, St. Francis, St. Agatha and Apollonia." The Virgin Mary and baby Jesus are being offered the pains of each martyr: St. Lucy offers her eyes on a platter, St. Agatha is giving them her cut-off breast, and Apollonia is showing the pliers with which her teeth were plucked out.

When we come back to Modena, Marina is baffled. "Why? Why would you ever go there?"

"We wanted to see the basilica and the cathedral in Reggio," I respond.

"But our cathedral is nicer, right?" she asks.

"I like them both," I say diplomatically, as though I'm a parent asked to decide on my favorite child.

"Vaffanculo!" Marina curses only half-jokingly. "Go live in Reggio then if you think it's so nice! Obviously, you like it better."

The Secret World of the Balsamic Vinegar Elite

Vinegar is not taken lightly in Modena. One store on the main street has a couple of very small bottles of the traditional *balsamico* in the window—behind bars—priced at $150. A weeklong vinegar conference features the mayor and food dignitaries from around Italy and the world.

Not until my second year living in Modena was I able to crack into the secret world of the vinegar elite and get a bottle for myself. I stumbled into this illustrious society when I made a grave error. I told Franco, the owner of the pet store in Vicolo Forni, about our Sunday drive up into the hills above Bologna with a couple of American friends. Once the words left my mouth, I wished I could have reached out and stuffed them back under my tongue. I blabbed to Franco how well we ate at a little *trattoria,* enjoying the delicious *crescentini,* a sort of flat bread, which we were told came from around Bologna. Franco was shocked and perhaps even a little offended. Fortunately he doesn't have a problem finding the right words, or as his wife says, "He likes to communicate."

Franco gently corrects me that *crescentini,* also known as *tigelle,* originate from the hills of Modena, not Bologna. Then he breaks into a smile. "The Bolognesi were lucky to have the good people from Modena next to them to teach them how to cook properly. If it weren't for us, they'd still be wearing animal skins and beating on drums."

And so my lesson in Modenese cuisine begins. Franco gestures to the huge covered market at the end of the alley and explains, "For example, it's difficult to find true vinegar inside there; it's only an industrialized imitation. If you come to my house this Sunday, I'll show you how the real balsamico is made in my acetaio," which he defines as a room with vinegar barrels.

I have already visited an industrial vinegar maker in Modena the year before, so I'm familiar with Modenese pride in their food. The man who led me around the little factory with industrial stainless-steel casks let me taste their very good approximation of the *tradizionale* balsamic. The company put dozens of different labels on the bottles of this vinegar to send all over the world. The guide then turned red with anger and told me, "Have you heard? Neapolitans are trying to steal our recipe! They're making cheap stuff with labels saying, 'Balsamic Vinegar from Modena, made in Napoli'!" He regained his composure about the vinegar fraud and assured me, "Anyway, it's impossible to make true balsamic vinegar anywhere but Modena." When I asked why, he replied, "Oh it's the air, the grapes, the humidity, everything."

In spite of his claim of authenticity for the industrial vinegar, this man showed me his own private, family *acetaio* with twenty barrels. I wiped away the cobwebs over the door, and he wiped a grubby window with his sleeve to let in a ray of light. "This is my mother!" he exclaimed with love as he pointed to a little cask in the corner. The "mother barrel" was full of the thick syrupy vinegar he claimed was more than a hundred years old. "I would never sell my mother. If the house catches on fire, it's the first thing we carry outside!"

This protectionist attitude toward the real *tradizionale* vinegar makes it almost impossible for a Modenese to part with it. In old times, *balsamico* was given as a priceless dowry and still today is usually exchanged as a gift since all the time and effort to produce the vinegar makes it far too expensive to buy.

An exchange student from the United States staying in Spilamberto, just outside of Modena and the real home of balsamic vinegar, was clandestinely offered vinegar by a high school classmate. Boys wanted to meet this beautiful young American girl but didn't know what to say to her. Finally one approached her, whispering romantically in her ear, "I can get you some *real* balsamic vinegar if you want." The American student couldn't have cared less about some dark, stinky vinegar; she was far more interested in meeting cute boys and having fun.

I have to find out how they make this precious elixir, so I jump at the chance to visit Franco's homemade vinegar setup. Franco and his wife, Giordana, pick Katy and me up early Sunday morning to take us for a breakfast of cappuccini and heart-stopping deep-fried dough called *gnocco fritto*. We then risk the dense fog of the Padana plains, driving dangerously fast to reach their house in the country and taste this Modenese elixir. Franco's nephew meets us at the door of the house, and Franco brings us some special *coppa* salami to taste. Franco's nephew doesn't want any. "Uncle, you know that I don't eat meat."

"What?" Franco shakes his head in mock dismay, "I don't understand why my own flesh and blood insists on being a vegetarian. We have the best pork in the world here, and all he wants to eat is salad!"

Franco's nephew tells us, "If I don't eat a bowl of tortellini every year at Christmastime, I'll be written out of the inheritance!"

After the pork products, we venture up to the little attic

of Franco's farmhouse to see a series of musty wooden barrels—each one smaller than the next—filling the room. The windows are wide open, and Franco explains, "Vinegar is alive and must be properly aged. Besides, I love it when the whole house has this fantastic odor of vinegar. It permeates everything!" he says, delighted. I'm sure we'll never be able to wash the acidic, molasses smell out of our clothes.

Franco describes the process to us, "Every November, Giordana and I boil a big batch of white Trebbiano wine to produce the fermented juice, or must. We add a little to the biggest barrel since almost a quarter of the liquid evaporates every year." Franco lifts a stone on top of this huge barrel, which seals a hole in the wooden slate. Nearly half of the rock is eaten away by the acid of the wine inside. I wonder what the vinegar must do to your stomach, but Franco assures me, "You need the acid, otherwise the vinegar would become a syrup."

Each barrel is made from a different type of wood—from juniper to chestnut—to give unique flavor to the black liquid. Once a year, the vinegar is decanted from the second smallest barrel into the mother barrel, from the third smallest into the second, and so on. Every year, an expert from the balsamic vinegar consortium, like a wine sommelier, tours the various *acetaia* (vinegar makers) to make sure the process is going as planned. "It's a very tense time," Franco tells me. "If you don't follow the process, your vinegar will be ruined. Ruined! Then you have to throw away all your bad vinegar, which was begun more than a hundred years ago. This is a disaster for the family." Franco drops his head sadly in sympathy for those who have lost all of their priceless liquid.

"After all this work, we produce only two liters a year, which we extract in January," Giordana cuts in when she sees Franco bow his head.

Franco recovers his gregarious manner and continues, "Now you can understand why no one wants to sell the real vinegar since we barely have enough for ourselves. For us Modenesi, we care a lot about preserving this tradition of balsamico, and I hope in the future someone will keep looking after my barrels to produce the real vinegar from Modena." I don't dare tell Franco that I heard a company in California is now trying to produce authentic balsamic vinegar also.

After the tour, Franco bestows upon us a tiny bottle of his dark brew. I carefully wrap paper around the four-ounce bottle of precious liquid to avoid any disastrous cracks or unnecessary shaking. Once we're back in the car, however, Franco guns the engine and swerves violently around the turns and joggles the vinegar, which nearly pops the puny cork.

We make it home safely, and the vinegar has survived. We can't resist the almost creamy sweet flavor of the vinegar, so we pour it on everything—from splinters of Parmigiano-Reggiano cheese to meats and even on desserts like fresh strawberries and gelato. The balsamic tang of the vinegar is addicting. As with any bad habit, the absence of the desired object leaves us wanting more.

Our neighbor upstairs, the little old lady with the two fat dogs, hears that we visited Franco's *acetaio*. "Now, you must try some balsamico from my barrels," she says and hands us a bigger bottle. Over the next week, we flatter both her and Franco (separately) that their vinegar is indeed the tastiest. "Just wait until next year's batch," Franco tells us.

Pet Pigs

E very day in Italy has a saint. In fact, there are not enough days in the year for all the saints. La Festa di San Antonio is today, and one of my students explains that many churches open their doors for owners to bring their pets to be blessed. Since she often speaks about her Siberian husky, which digs holes in her garden, I ask if she's going to bring her dog to Mass.

"My dog needs all the blessing he can get! Unfortunately, he eats cats," she admits. "We've found two dead cats in our yard recently. The priests say the church has a calming effect on the animals, but I wouldn't want him to start eating other people's cats during Mass."

I call up my friend Antonio, who I used to believe was a spy. He accepts my best wishes for his "name day," the day of the saint after whom he's named, which is nearly as important as a birthday in Italy. Most people have no idea of the holy deeds of their namesake, except, of course, Antonio, because his saint is always pictured with a piglet by his side. For this special occasion, I give Antonio a can of Spam imported from America, which he can add to his collection of pig objects.

Antonio invites me to the dinner event he's planning. I can't help rolling my eyes, but I am insanely curious nevertheless. His recent bizarre feats have been "Parfum de Porceau," a pig perfume for "the man who doesn't need to ask," and "Vin de Porc," a Lambrusco for "the man who doesn't want to wait." I'm dying to know what his next shenanigan will be.

"Grunci the trained pig is going to ring in New Year's in Riccione," Antonio tells me. Antonio is planning a New Year's Eve party to take place in November so the television media can film it and air it December 31.

Katy and I meet Antonio in front of the city hall of the resort town of Riccione, where he has displayed all his pig souvenirs. He's there with Grunci's owners, Elisa and Mauro, who appear in matching blue and yellow jogging suits with the words "Dog City" written across their chests. They run a kennel where people leave their dogs while they're on vacation. With so many dogs around, their pig now assumes he's a dog as well.

They pull Grunci out of the back of their station wagon and stroll him along the boardwalk amid the elite vacationers on the way to the restaurant.

"Mother of God, what the fuck is that?!" says a young, well-dressed hipster when he sees the pig on a leash.

"I don't know. It looks like a wild boar or something!" replies his friend.

Grunci's owners constantly have to explain he's not a wild boar but an American dwarf pig from Texas.

Another woman strutting around in a full-length mink and gabbing on her cell phone drags along her disgruntled child by his sleeve. The kid escapes to run over to pet Grunci. The disgusted mother again yanks her *bambino* away from the pig and says something about sterilizing his hands when they get home.

When we arrive at the restaurant, the diners are either shocked or intrigued to see a pig enter. "It's OK," Antonio assures me. "I called ahead, and they said it's fine if we bring our trained pig." The owners welcome our large group, but I'm confident the health department would do otherwise.

As we munch on prosciutto before the meal, children flock around Grunci as overly protective mothers pull them away. An enormous man bends down next to the relatively small pig to have his picture taken.

I offer Antonio some of the fantastic ham that is being passed around. He refuses. "I never touch the stuff!" he exclaims. "I'm a vegetarian, you know." I wonder if Antonio is a sort of spy after all—an undercover animal rights activist. After a couple of glasses of Lambrusco, he reveals to me he couldn't resist opening the can of Spam I gave him. "I just had to try it," he says. "It didn't taste very good, though." He tells me he didn't heat it up and just ate it with a spoon right out of the can.

While waiting for pizzas, I ask Grunci's owners if they have any other pets, besides the dogs they house at the kennel. "I had a kitty, but one of the neighbors was always admiring it," the wife, Elisa, tells me. "One day, the cat was missing. The neighbor abducted the poor cat and ate it."

I've heard eating cats was common in the war but can't imagine my cat, Sven, on my plate with an apple in his mouth. Rumor has it that Vicenza is famous for serving cat, so I asked a friend from Vicenza if this was true. "Oh no! That's such a lie," she responded, a little offended. "In fact, I've only eaten cat once in my life." Supposedly all rabbits and chickens in butcher shops have to have their heads still attached so sneaky butchers won't substitute alley cats. I still don't understand why somebody would willingly eat a cat.

As Grunci nuzzles us for some treats, I express my condolences to Elisa for her cat—in between bites of delicious prosciutto—and tell her I can't believe someone would eat a pet. Grunci's male owner, Mauro, shrugs and says with his mouth full, "I'd eat cat, or dog even, if it was cooked properly." He doesn't seem too worried about saying this even though he runs a kennel for dogs. Elisa looks at him and says, "You'd eat anything; you're such a pig!"

Meanwhile, Antonio has started giving a speech since it's nearly midnight. He tells the small crowd he wants to write a biography of Grunci, as the little pig gnaws on napkins, people's pant legs, and anything else he can get his snout on. Grunci chews on the tablecloth and nearly pulls off a pile of plates.

Grunci's owners pass around a feature in a major Italian magazine that recently ran about their trained pig. Antonio has publicized the New Year's event with Grunci, so a group of photographers starts snapping pictures of the pig and the clock Antonio has set up behind him. I quietly ask Antonio how Grunci will know when it's midnight. He looks at me like I just don't get it. "Oh, he won't. He's just a pig, you know. We'll pull his tail or something to make him squeal. Then the press will think he's truly smart!"

At that moment, the clock strikes midnight, and Antonio pokes the pig to make him squeal. Flashbulbs blind everyone as we marvel at this very intelligent animal, and Antonio revels in the limelight with Grunci.

Buon Natale!

The couple at the *tabacchi,* or tobacconist's, are always thrilled to see us. Usually, the gregarious clerk and her husband say *"ciao"* no less than eight times before and after I buy stamps for a postcard. Even after I shut the door behind me, they are still wishing me a good day. As Christmas approaches, they have a whole new list of greetings to give: *Auguri! Auguroni! Buon Natale! E anche Buon Anno!* (Best wishes! Very best wishes! Merry Christmas! And also Happy New Year!").

Any Italian grammar book teaches that formal situations call for the greetings *buon giorno* or *buona sera.* Although Italian is a melodious language, somehow these greetings are often dutifully expressed in a bored, formal monotone as though all life has been sucked out of the speaker. Such a simple welcome would never suffice for the talkative people of Emilia. Although this monotonous *buon giorno* exists in Modena, much more common is an animated *Ciao! Buon giorno! Salve! Ciao, ciao! ciao!* (Hi! Good day! Greetings! Hi, hi! hi!).

Also, when leaving, Italians seldom say *addio* ("bye," or literally "to God") since it insinuates you're going away forever, essentially dying. Instead, they think positively about when you'll see each other again: *Arrivederci! Buon giorno! Buon weekend! Ci vediamo presto! Ciao, ciao, ciao!* (Until we see you again! Good day! Have a good weekend! See you soon! Bye, bye, bye!).

At Christmas, we plan a few extra minutes for greetings at each stop in the market since every vendor bids us, "Auguri! Auguroni! Buon Natale! E anche Buon Anno!" No longer will the usual string of hellos suffice, and a simple "ciao!" seems almost rude.

The bum in Vicolo Forni has caught the Christmas spirit and puts on a red velvet hat with white and gold trim. Attracted by his bushy gray beard and hearty Yuletide greetings, little kids in strollers reach out to him and say, "Ciao, Babbo Natale!" (Hi, Father Christmas!). The mothers steer their toddlers the other direction but are obliged to give him a half euro. The bum doesn't disappoint, however; he dances a little jig each time more money jingles in his pocket. His Kris Kringle act loses a little appeal when he tips up his box wine and red droplets drizzle down his front. Regardless, it's the holidays, so I give him a mini *pandoro* Christmas bread.

While the bum is enjoying his pre-Christmas feast, I'm trying to teach an English lesson in my apartment directly above where he's usually stationed. It's December 8, and one of my students wishes me a happy *Festa della Madonna,* which he loosely translates as a "Virgin Party." I can't imagine this is exactly what he means, so he explains that today is the day the Virgin Mary heard from the angel Gabriel that she was pregnant with God's child. Not being well versed in Scripture, I tell him I'm surprised she could get pregnant and give birth in the same month. "It's a miracle, of course," he says, then whispers, "I think it was Joseph all along, but they couldn't tell their parents."

Besides these blasphemous thoughts, another sacred cow is being poisoned: *pandoro* Christmas bread. The *telegiornale* evening news has a lead story about a rally against genetically modified food. A group of environmentalists had a press conference in which they put a few drops of hazardous chemicals into a *pandoro* loaf to show how supposedly "toxic" it is. After all, what would Christmastime be in Italy without a protest? Terror strikes the country as rumors spread that *pandoro* has been tainted by dangerous tree huggers. While the *pandoro* producers try to calm the public and the environmentalists try to explain themselves, the public doesn't listen and curses them both. Maybe it's just my imagination, but the bum seems to be giving me nasty looks for giving him the mini *pandoro*.

I stop at the newspaper to wish Roberto a *Buon Natale*, but he's enraptured by his new toy, a Furby-talking stuffed animal. He cuddles it and rocks it to sleep. Not many articles are being written today as he gathers the staff around to see how cute it is when he wakes up his Furby by activating its motion detector. I show Roberto the singing fish toy that we brought back from the United States, and he sets up his Furby doll to be triggered by the fish.

Back in Vicolo Forni, Maurizio is decorating his bar, Il Cappuccino, with strings of lights. We stop down to show him our singing fish toy. He is so impressed he gathers the regulars into the tiny bar to look at this "great American discovery." Maurizio begs us to get him one and jokes, "That's why you Americans are so far ahead of the rest of the world. Where else would people think of something like this?"

Although we consider giving the singing fish to the bum just to watch him dance with it on Vicolo Forni, we end up giving it to Maurizio for his three-year-old son for Christmas. He reports back that they put the fish up on the wall in the kitchen, but his son likes it so much he climbs onto the table to push the button and make the fish sing. The toddler dances nonstop and eventually Maurizio has to hide the fish under his bed. He now curses this infernal American invention.

Christmas crèche scenes have popped up everywhere, and Franco, who gave us a tour of his balsamic vinegar room, even has a little baby Jesus in his fishbowl in his pet store window. Guido tells us Naples has an art school dedicated solely to making crèches. Children peer into toy shop windows along the Via Emilia coveting the precious crèche figurines and hoping they can fill out their collection at home.

A life-size manger scene is set up in the piazza, and Christmas shoppers stop and exclaim, "Che bello!" (How beautiful!). Personally, I'm much more impressed with the forty-foot-tall pine tree hauled into the center of the piazza than with the plastic Bible characters, but I'm obviously in the minority. Christmas trees are an imported tradition, and now little evergreens are on every corner.

Ornate strands of lights are strung over the streets and provide the perfect backdrop for the choir singing holiday carols in dialect. Although the streets are pedestrian-only, that doesn't stop a buzzing scooter from interrupting the songs. The singers move aside without missing a note to let the impatient scooterist through. While I'm annoyed, everyone else has a much better Christmas spirit, and no one so much as gives a dirty look to the law-breaking scooter.

Busy shoppers stop at the sweets booths set up on the streets to buy candy canes, Sicilian *torrone* nougat, and a black hard candy with which they intend to trick their naughty little ones by stuffing their stockings with what looks like coal. Finally, a far-too-thin Santa Claus appears tooling down the Via Emilia, but in place of eight reindeer, his sleigh is pulled through the crowd by a three-wheeled Vespa car. The children all wave to Babbo Natale as he shouts, "Auguri! Ciao! Saluti! Buon Natale e Buon Anno! Auguroni! Ciao, ciao, ciao!"

Sunny Italy

The A1 *autostrada* is known as the Highway of the Sun because it leads to the balmy climate of southern Italy. Today, on Christmas Eve, it's an enormous parking lot as far as the eye can see. Katy and I are scrunched into the backseat of Sonia's dad's car, and we've been completely stopped for about half an hour now. Many of the cars have turned off their engines, and a man has even gotten out of his car to walk his dog next to the road. A few other people are in the grass, having a picnic of prosciutto and wine, while waiting for the cars to start moving. When the traffic begins crawling again, people scramble into their cars. Suddenly, the road opens up, and cars speed up to 150 kilometers per hour and then screech to a sudden stop when they see another line of halted cars, probably due to another accident. Sonia and her dad declare that it's time for another break.

Our friend Sonia has invited us to spend Christmas at her grandmother's house in the hills of southern Italy above the Greek ruins at Paestum. Each one of these hill towns has its own dialect and would be completely isolated if it weren't for salt. During the Middle Ages, these villages were self-sufficient except for the need to trade their goods for salt. When Italy was united, the government controlled the salt industry to stop battles fought for salt and to impose a stiff tax. The old "T" signs at the *tabacchi* list their two products as tobacco and salt. Salt was once such a precious commodity that spilling the shaker at the table was a grave error. To be forgiven, toss a pinch over your shoulder or else your soul will haunt the house forever!

These remote villages are notoriously superstitious. I spent a month in a hill town in the province of Lazio where the townsfolk were convinced a rich werewolf roamed the alleyways. A small boy told me the story with fear in his eyes about the *licantropo* (lycanthrope) who lived in a big house at the edge of town. Every full moon, he would stalk the town in search of water. Everyone would lock the doors and bolt the shutters as this man howled through the streets with a pack of stray dogs nervously following him but keeping their distance. The werewolf would go from one fountain to the next but could never quench his thirst. Some people would leave bottles of water out for him, which would be empty in the morning. The story ended anticlimactically, however, when the boy told me, "To solve his problem, the rich werewolf installed a pool in his backyard. Now when the full moon comes, he just takes a swim."

I asked the little boy if fear of werewolves was the reason that old ladies dumped buckets of water on my friends and me when we were on the streets late at night. He looked at me like I was crazy and replied, "No, that's because you were loud."

A friend's grandmother at another remote hill town remembered when her village was ruled by an evil Albanian baron. He refused to let his town join the rest of the united Italy, and the government had better things to do than lay siege to the tiny fortified hill town. The grandmother remembered that people working in the fields would bow in the dirt when he passed on his horse and never dare look at him. If he wasn't satisfied with their work, he'd haul them

into his castle and fling them out into the fields with a cata-
pult. One day he died on his porcelain toilet—the only one
in town—but everyone, including his servants, were so
afraid of him they wouldn't go into the bathroom. He was
there for a week.

Getting to these little towns is not easy. To get to Piag-
giane, the town where Sonia's grandmother lives, her dad
drives us eight hours from Modena, crammed into a tiny
car in a traffic jam along with every southern Italian who
works in the north and vacations in the south. We have
pizza in Salerno south of Naples, but then hop in the car
again for another two hours of twisting and turning up into
the mountains. At this point, our legs are numb and stomachs nauseated.

We enter the hill town and see large fires raging in each
little square. "We have bonfires every Christmas Eve to warm
the town for the coming of the new baby Jesus," Sonia tells
us. Her dad parks the car, and we walk to be warmed by
the bonfires in the piazzas. People risk standing close to the
flames because the temperature in this mountain town is
close to freezing. Kids lob huge firecrackers into the flames,
which explode with a flurry of sparks, and the parents chase
after the irreverent rascals. The bonfires nearly block the
roads, so cars navigate dangerously close and sometimes
even skim the burning logs. I'm not quite as brave as everyone else and stand back in case there's an even bigger explosion from a little Fiat with a full tank of gas.

We meet some of Sonia's friends next to the fires, and
one tells us in English, "I want to take you to my house and
make you drink wine and eat spaghetti." We take a rain
check, but he leads us to the town church, which will be re-
opened at midnight for the first time since renovation after
the latest earthquake. The townspeople invested in fireworks

to celebrate the event, so everyone has packed into the street in front of the church. The bells of the steeple peal at twelve midnight, and the blasts begin. Only the children are unafraid of the bombs; everyone else runs for cover in doorways or behind steps. The smoke has nowhere to go and soon fills the narrow street, causing the revelers to cough and put handkerchiefs over their mouths. To escape the fumes, people rush into the church, where we watch a big-screen TV with a live satellite link to the Pope giving his Christmas blessing in Rome.

Exhausted from traveling all day, we go back to Sonia's grandmother's little home. The stone house is frigid inside, so they let us sleep in the cozy living room by a tiny fireplace. To be extra hospitable, our bed has two mattresses. When we lie down on the soft pads stacked on top of each other, we sink down a good eight inches and can't move. Luckily nothing can stop us from falling sound asleep.

Everyone else is up early on Christmas morning, but we don't want to get out of our nice warm beds. Finally, Katy goes to the bathroom, and Sonia's family immediately comes into our bedroom, the living room, and lights the fire. This little fireplace is the only heat source for the entire house, so they all huddle around to warm up. Sonia shows me around the house, and when we go into the attic, I understand why the house is so cold. The red tile roof keeps the water off, but the round shape of the shingles lets light in, and the heat slips out. In the old days the openings were necessary for the big brick oven in the corner of the attic, which was used to cook bread and pizza and even to smoke meats and cheese. The wood oven inside the home had been a sign of wealth since the grandmother didn't have to use the communal oven in the center of town every day.

Sonia's grandmother is dressed in black, as are all the widows in town. She jokes that on Christmas day the old ladies pay little kids to kiss their wrinkly hands to bring them good luck. She wants to visit a nearby grotto where a statue of the Madonna appeared but couldn't possibly have fit through the opening of the cave. "How did it get there?" I ask. *Un miracolo!* (a miracle), we're told. Before she goes out, she points at us and tells Sonia's mother to make sure "the guests eat a lot." We've been overfed the entire time. Katy and I feel rude to refuse the constant offerings, but after a while we're so stuffed we have no choice but to stop eating. In spite of our "no, thank you's," sandwiches, candy, bananas, nuts, and other treats appear in front of us all day, and Sonia's mom looks at us expectantly. We realize our fatal mistake was eating these snacks after we politely declined. They must think that we *facciamo i complimenti,* meaning we say "no" to everything because we don't want to impose.

To recover from the abundance of food, we take a walk to the piazza. The embers from last night's bonfires still heat the streets and fend off the impending winter cold. We stop to get a cappuccino in Il Bar Cavallino, where Ferrari stickers are stuck all over the windows and bar. The people at the bar refuse to let us pay and insist on offering us the coffee; they even give us a brioche since they know we're the guests of Sonia's family. Although we are still full from breakfast, at their insistence we eat every bite of the flaky, buttery brioche.

We're stuffed and hope that we can take a nap back at Sonia's grandmother's house. When we open the door, we're escorted to the table because it's time for lunch. Sonia's dad pops open a bottle of champagne, and the festivities begin. Her mother brings out two giant pans of lasagne that she stuffed full of everything in the fridge, including hot dogs. "I'm not a very good cook," she confesses.

What she may lack in culinary prowess, she makes up for in quantity. Katy is served a giant piece of lasagne as big as her head. "Adesso mangia!" (Now eat!) the mother says. We look at everyone else's plates and find that we're served twice as much. With all eyes on us, we struggle through the lasagne and try to keep smiling through the pain in our stomachs.

"Now it is time for the goat!" the grandmother proclaims. A giant tray of the traditional Christmas dish of baby goat is proudly placed on the table. The meat looks delicious, but I'm physically incapable of eating any more food. As we poke at the kid meat pathetically with our forks, the grandmother looks at us disappointed and pours us some more of the delicious local red wine. Although most women in Italy don't drink, the grandmother has a tumbler full of this hearty wine. She claims it gives her strength. Obviously we're doing something wrong, because the wine knocks us out, but not before we endure the pain of eating the goat. Fortunately, a long Christmas nap is also a tradition.

The next day, the grandmother tells us she's glad no babies were born yesterday because giving birth on Christmas day produces monsters. These seemingly normal babies will turn into demons every Christmas. To stop these little beasts as they go stalking through town, everyone leaves a broom outside their door, so the monsters get distracted by counting the strands. When I ask her why, she answers, "That's just what monsters do; they count broom strands!"

Even though it's only 7:30 in the morning, she's going to catch the bus to go to her son's house to slaughter a pig. The day after Christmas, Saint Steven's day, is pig-killing day, and she claims to be the only one in the family who knows how to do it properly. After they butcher the animal, they're going to spend the day stuffing intestines to make sausages. In the evening they celebrate by eating pig's blood pudding. We're welcome to join her but politely opt for a bit of sightseeing instead.

Getting into the car to drive around in the mountains, we run into one of Sonia's friends. When we explain we're going to Laurino, a striking hill town nearby, he wonders what's wrong with his town and jokes semi-seriously, "Why would you ever want to go there? What do they have that we don't?"

After Laurino, we drive into a cold ghost town high in the mountains, and Sonia explains this town was sliding down the hillside, so everyone had to leave. One woman stubbornly stayed in her house and refused to leave, even after the government told her that the slightest earthquake would cause the abandoned town to slip down hundreds of feet into the valley.

Although we came south to experience the warmth of Italy, these towns are frigid in winter. Hardly anyone's house is heated, so we bundle up in the car to stay warm. We search through our Italy guidebook and discover that the island of Ischia has hot thermal springs. We're not only full of food but freezing cold, in spite of the fact that we're from Minnesota, and are forced to escape the cold of southern Italy.

The Hot Springs of Ischia

Getting to the island of Ischia is no easy task. Lugging heavy backpacks through downtown Naples is not the ideal way to sightsee this densely populated city, so we head straight for the ferry. Although some boat trips have been canceled due to the rough waves, our captain risks it.

Once out at sea, we understand why many ships are staying docked in Naples. Our boat bounces like a basketball, so we ask at the bar if they have any motion sickness pills. "No, those can only be sold at pharmacies." Instead, plastic bags are passed around on deck to stop people from retching off the side of the ferry. We have to look away as whole families spend their vacation around garbage cans losing their lunch.

An hour and a half later, the barf boat enters the port of Ischia. To get to our hotel, we hop on an oversized bus, which navigates the tiny, windy roads of this volcanic island at top speed. Large vehicles must stop a half mile from our destination, so with relief we leave the bus and walk the last leg down into the picturesque town of Sant'Angelo. At sunset, we traverse the isthmus to our little hotel dug into the rocks. The red and orange light of the sunset illuminates the colorful houses perched on the cliffs as the waves gently lap on the shore. The beauty of the seaside town fills our eyes with pleasure, and suddenly the difficult trip was all worthwhile.

Our room has no heat, but it doesn't matter, since the next day we're on our way to the volcanic hot springs. The wind blows hard, and the waves are even rougher than the day before. In our bathrobes and sandals, we walk up the narrow path along the cliff to the thermal baths high above town, determined to get warm.

The hot water is heated by the magma deep below the island, bubbling as though the whole little paradise of Ischia is ready to explode. All the naturally heated pools are perched on the rocky cliffs overlooking the Mediterranean, which stretches into the distance until it meets the sky. Intricate tile designs surround the pools, which come in all shapes and temperatures to satisfy the handful of visitors. Our favorites are the *grotte romane*—the Roman caves—that are carved into the sides of the cliff face. We walk down a rock path with irregular steps cut out of the edge of the precipice. A shaky railing keeps us from plunging into the waves a hundred feet below, but the reward is worth the danger. We bend down to squeeze into the steamy caves filled with the hot water that we've sought. We lie in the calm caves high above the sea and hear the angry wind blustering outside. We're safe and warm.

After a couple hours of soaking, we peer out of our caves to find that the waves below are now crashing fifteen feet high against the rocks. We pull our waterlogged bodies out of the caves and brave the wind to go back to the larger pools. The wind has thrown the beach chairs into a chaotic pile, and flower pots crash from the balconies. We meet a man from Milan at the hot springs who asks the receptionist why they don't put their plants inside so they don't break. "Ah, it's OK. We'll clean up tomorrow," she responds calmly.

No one seems too concerned with these stormy conditions, so we assume that this is just a windy place with giant waves. We get dressed to walk down the hill back into town. As we stroll back on the path along the cliff in our flip-flops, we have to hold on tight to a guard rail to not be blown off. The restaurants along the edge of the cliff are being destroyed by the waves, and the windows are smashed, with glass everywhere. Nobody is bothering to clean up. A man sticks his head out of his door and is shocked to see us. We can't hear him over the wind but understand when he emphatically gestures for us to run.

Although his intentions are good, we lose control as soon as we start running. The wind catches our backs and pushes us along so we can't stop. We barely manage to grab onto a door knob to stop being blown away just as the roof is blown off one of the buildings. Hand over hand, holding on to the wall of the building, we make it into a café. The alleys in town have been turned into wind tunnels, and we hear that someone broke his arm from being pushed around by the wind.

We tell the people in the bar we have to get across the long isthmus to our hotel. The men in the bar say, "We've never seen anything like this before, but you can probably make it across." They step outside to watch us try to cross, but we're blown back and barely grab onto another building. They laugh as we come crawling, literally, back to the café. One of them calls up our hotel across the isthmus and tells the receptionist, "We have a couple of your American guests here. They just about blew to Capri!"

A man from the hotel picks us up in his car, and we speed across the isthmus dodging boulders on the little road. Sand and waves batter the car, and the driver admits even he's scared. All the electricity is out in the hotel, so we eat some crackers by candlelight for dinner.

The next morning, the winds have completely stopped. Kids are playing on the isthmus and trying to ride on a poor dog, a boxer about double their size. A man walks along the shore with a basket collecting fish that have washed up on the beach.

The damage from yesterday's storm is being assessed. A ferry anchored in the port nearby broke one of its two chains and began going around in circles, ruining all the wooden boats nearby. Apparently, leaving Ischia is going to be as difficult as arriving was, but at least we got warm for a few brief hours in the hot springs.

Naples at New Year's

"Naples is probably the most beautiful city in Italy," many of my northern Italian friends who have been there tell me. Others, who have only heard television reports from the south, immediately make gestures of people stealing, being handcuffed and tossed in the clink. "Just be careful they don't trick you!" they say as they pull down slightly on their eyelid to make the gesture of *furbo*.

I admit I'm a little nervous to visit Naples since I spent one night there about ten years ago. Outside my hotel room near the train station, I heard some yelling and five gunshots during the middle of the night. When I tell Guido and his Neapolitan friends, they joke, "They do that for the tourists!"

Naples is the legendary New Year's spot because most families invest hundreds, sometimes thousands, of dollars in fireworks. The better the party, the better the coming year will be. "Vesuvius is going to explode! Vesuvius is going to explode!" is the rumor spreading like wildfire this year because a group of Neapolitan pyrotechnic masters want to make the volcano seem like it's blowing sky-high in the largest fireworks display ever.

Danger and miracles are commonplace in Naples, as shown by the supersaturated blood of the patron saint San Gennaro, which incredibly turns from solid to liquid every year. For good luck at New Year's, superstitious Neapolitans believe in "out with the old and in with the new." Many people save their old or broken plates to toss out the window, and for extra good luck they toss old appliances. Walking on the street below is like walking under an avalanche of last year's household goods.

In spite of these unusual traditions, Neapolitans are famous for their ability to live it up and enjoy life. Even so, northern prejudice runs strongly against southern Italy. I heard it the first time at a soccer game in Brescia, when all the *tifosi* fans chanted, "Dal Po in giù l'Italia non c'è più!" (South of the Po River, there's no more Italy!). According to this view, a small sliver of the north is the only "real" Italy, and even northern cities like Bologna, Parma, and Florence would essentially be considered Africa.

Almost everything we Americans consider to be "Italian" comes from the south: opera, pizza, pasta, meatballs, mozzarella, Mafia, espresso, vendettas, protective brothers when you look at their sisters, and so on. Northern Italians become furious when they come to the United States and are confronted with these stereotypes.

Guido invited Katy and me to stay at his mother's house in Naples for New Year's; he thinks the post office will give him time off since he put in a request in October. Back in Modena, Katy and I prepared for the trip to Naples by stopping in Piazza Maggiore in Bologna to buy a map of Italy. On closer inspection, the map is of "La Padania," which includes northern Italy but ends below the central regions of Umbria and Le Marche. The woman at the stand told me, "This will be the name of our new country once we secede from the south." I told her I thought the secessionists believed the north begins above the Po River. She shrugged off my comments. "We decided to include Tuscany and Umbria since they're both so beautiful." I examined the short map and realized once we're south of Umbria, we're on our own.

When I asked what's south of "Padania," she told me, "We like to call that other country 'Terronia' because it's full of 'Terroni.'" I thought this meant "terrorist," but I found out it comes from *terra*, which means "earth." *Terroni* are people who work on the earth, or farmers, and *Terronia* would mean "nation of the earth." Sounds good to me and definitely better than all the pollution and factories of the north.

Guido drives south early in his little red Fiat to celebrate Christmas with his family, and we take the boat back from the island of Ischia to Naples. Seeing the city by the bay, I think it's no wonder the Greeks set up their new colony here. The sun shimmers on the water of the bay, and the silhouette of Vesuvius continually threatens the metropolis.

Guido's mother meets us at the port and explains that Guido has to stay back at her house. His boss wouldn't give him the time off from work, but he came to Naples anyway. He's been calling in sick for an entire week and has to send a certified letter every day to the post office in Modena from a doctor—who is a friend of the family. Even so, Guido has to stay home from ten to twelve in the morning and four to six in afternoon in case his boss sends a special state-employed doctor to check if he's really ill.

At the apartment, Guido is in his bathrobe sitting in front of the TV. He says he feels sick now. His *mamma* has been feeding him, and he's eaten too much, so he can do little else but sit on the couch. "Look at me," he says patting his stomach. "I look pregnant!" I ask if he's worried about losing his job, and he replies, "No, even if they catch me, I don't think they can really fire me. It would take years for them to process all the paperwork. It's much more trouble than it's worth."

The first thing to do upon entering Naples is to eat a real Neapolitan pizza. It's noon, so Guido can escape his home for a while because the doctor can't make a surprise inspection at lunchtime—some things are sacred. He takes Katy and me to a famous pizzeria where you eat standing up in the street. When Bill Clinton was president, he came here and folded the pizza in quarters and ate it; everyone cheered and took photos because he knew how the locals do it. Guido shows me the proper technique, and I manage to eat mine the same way. Nobody gives a damn—at least I don't need the Secret Service on every side of me.

For dessert, I sink my teeth into a *sfogliatelle*, a pastry stuffed with ricotta that is supposedly made by nuns. It falls apart into thousands of crumbs all over my shirt. The *barista* then serves up steaming hot espresso—only about a tablespoon in the bottom of a tiny *tazza*. With that half mouthful of pure caffeine, we're sufficiently wired to drive.

Guido zooms his little red Fiat through Naples in search of *fuochi artificiali* (literally "artificial fire," meaning fireworks). The ride is far better than any roller coaster because none of the traditional rules of the road apply in Napoli. I read in the newspaper that a new scandal erupted in Naples about people cheating on their driver's test. Tiny microphones were mounted in their shirt collars, and they would read the question under their breath. A person in another room listened and responded with a little remote-controlled device that sent a vibration to the tester of one for true, two for false. I showed the article to Guido, who was impressed by the ingenuity of the scheme.

Guido advises me that illegal drivers are just one of the reasons why driving in Naples is so exciting. As we blast through town, I take notes on driving in Naples, thanks to Guido:

1. *Only go through traffic lights when the light is red.* Running red lights has become so common that everything is backward. If you dare go through when the light's green, look both ways, flash your lights, and honk your horn.

2. *If someone bumps you from behind, for heaven's sake, don't stop!* The Camorra, Naples's home-bred Mafia, has a new ploy for carjacking, which has led to even more hit-and-runs. Think of the streets as a big smash-up derby.

3. *Passing on the right.* You can do anything to get past all those cars in front of you. If there's no room, use the sidewalk. Around blind corners, just honk and go. Especially dangerous curves are indicated with flowers and crosses.

4. *Don't drive a "foreign" car in Naples.* License plates from other parts of Italy are considered fair game in Naples to steal, smash, or otherwise damage. The same applies, however, for cars with a Neapolitan license plate outside Naples.

5. *Don't expect anyone else to have insurance.* Always have pen and paper ready to write down license plate numbers, but many people don't have their license plates on their cars.

6. *Follow that ambulance!* The only way through backed-up traffic is to stay right on the tail of an ambulance with its siren blaring and lights flashing.

7. *Never wash your car.* Never fix dents in your car; it's less likely to be stolen. Never park a new car outside overnight, unless you generously tip the suspicious-looking person watching over the parking lot.

8. *"My horn is broken, so I can't drive my car,"* my friend Anna once told me. Although this seemed ridiculous, the danger of not leaning on your horn at all times in Naples is tantamount to taking a snooze on railroad tracks. Besides, if you were to have an accident (and the other driver didn't speed away), the judge would rule against you because your car would be considered broken.

9. *Show no fear, and never wear your seat belt.* Other drivers sense your dread of dying at the wheel, and in that moment of hesitation, they'll sneak in front of you. As a passenger, never fasten your seat belt unless the driver does; it's an insult to their ability to drive. If you're worried about cops pulling you over for breaking the seat belt law, buy one of the new T-shirts dreamed up by a wily Neapolitan with a fake seat belt silk-screened across the front to foil the fuzz.

10. *Beware of cars with newspaper covering the windows.* Discreet Neapolitan sweethearts who can't afford a hotel squeeze into their tiny Fiats for a little backseat gymnastics and line the windshield with yesterday's *Il Corriere della Sera* for some privacy. Be careful not to bump into these four-wheel love dens. One reckless driver did just that when a couple of lovers were near the crucial point of no return. Their secret rendezvous was revealed, and the lovers sued since the woman became pregnant.

After numerous near-death experiences, Guido finds his target. On all corners of Naples around New Year's, street urchins known as *scugnizzi* playfully toss huge firecrackers at pedestrians—especially at nervous Americans like me. No one scolds them. Neapolitans accept the explosions underfoot as part of the festivities. Fireworks stands are set up around the city and are advertised by setting off rounds of explosions in the street while cars dodge the shrapnel. The biggest illegal firecrackers are not on display but are hidden beneath the sparklers and lady fingers in a box under the table. For the truly powerful bombs—which in the United States we would call dynamite—a reservation is required. Teenagers tend most of the stands since jail sentences are far less for kids if the *carabinieri* discover their explosives are contraband.

It's New Year's Eve, and the newscast announces that the *carabinieri* found a whole shipment of bombs as big as grapefruits hidden under a crate of oranges headed for northern Italy. In Naples, almost all of the homemade fireworks would be classified as terrorist bombs, but the police know there's no way to stop it. My Neapolitan friends say it's the same thing every year and may even be the same video footage shown on the news in the past. Last year, explosive entrepreneurs built the *"Bomba Maradona"* measuring the size of a loaf of bread in honor of their favorite ex-football player, Diego Maradona. I wonder what the *carabinieri* are going to do with all of their seized goods tomorrow night—probably have a little celebration of their own.

Seba, Guido's friend who works at the *questura*, is home for the holidays and invites us to supper at his girlfriend's apartment. The mandatory menu is spaghetti and clams. The price of mussels and clams has skyrocketed for New Year's, so makeshift stands have been set up on street corners to sell black-market shellfish.

Another Italian tradition for New Year's is *zampone* with lentils. Fortunately, we can skip the heavy pork because we get enough of that in Modena. Instead of the lentils, which supposedly make you rich, we each munch on a date and put a seed in our wallet. They assure me that this will make us rich year-round.

While enjoying the delicious meal, I see the apartment windows tremble as enormous explosions light the streets outside and cause car alarms to blare nonstop. I feel like I'm in Bosnia or Baghdad, trying to ignore the blasts. Although it's only eight o'clock, everyone at the table is disappointed. "Last year, there were many more explosions."

When I suggest going out to see the fireworks, Guido is amazed at my stupidity. "People drop bombs down on the street. You can't go outside now!" Instead, we go up on the roof six stories above the street with a panorama of Naples and a view of Vesuvius ready to explode. Armed with a small supply of fireworks and a few bottles of spumante champagne, we have the perfect spot to stay until midnight.

The countdown to midnight begins: *cinque, quattro, tre, due, uno,* and then the city explodes. Roman candles shoot sparks from every balcony, as though flaming gas leaks are shooting out of each building. Huge blasts on the street shake entire buildings and light up the whole town for an instant. I try to look up, but whistling bottle rockets are dropping sparks all around. Supposedly the Camorra shoot their handguns into the air, but with all this racket, no one would notice.

After five minutes of nearly continuous blasts, smoke covers the city and obscures the view. Everyone who parked their car on the street is worried about finding blast marks on their paint job and hopes not to find a stove embedded in the roof, dropped by a luckless neighbor. We hear on the news that drivers who decided it was better to take a spin into town to avoid falling fridges and see the fireworks ended up blocked in traffic until five in the morning.

I don't think Vesuvius actually exploded, but I'm not sure, because the imposing volcano is hidden by the haze. Hours afterwards, smoke from gunpowder still covers Naples, and champagne corks and garbage hide the streets. Bomb squads roam the streets looking for unexploded firecrackers before the street sweepers get an unpleasant surprise.

The next day, headlines of the newspaper blare that two people are dead and more than one hundred are injured from fireworks in Naples alone. "That's nothing; last year four were killed," Guido tells me.

Even with these tragedies, it seems everyone had the party of their lives. The volcano didn't really blow up. Apparently that was another Neapolitan exaggeration. Even so, Naples after New Year's does resemble Pompeii after the eruption.

San Geminiano and the Festival of Fog

Back in Modena, the lines stretched all the way out the doors of the cathedral to see the bones of San Geminiano, the town's patron saint. Roberto told me that the legend says that Attila the Hun and his troops were coming down through Italy, so San Geminiano performed the miracle of covering Modena in fog. Forever after, the town has been in debt to San Geminiano (and covered with haze).

The mist settles over the plains of the Po Valley for months, and everybody accepts the fact that half of the town is out with *l'influenza* or *la febbre* (fever). Visibility gets down to about thirty feet, but that doesn't stop drivers from zipping along on the *autostrada* highway at full tilt. This white-knuckle driving is petrifying. Don't go too slowly because the guy tailgating will bash you from behind. Pileups of more than two hundred cars crashing into each other occur at least once a winter, mostly because someone decided to slow down while a Ferrari driver couldn't resist gunning it through the fog.

The last day of January, in the thick of winter, Modenesi celebrate the fog by revealing the holy bones for the only time of the year. Frightened children are dragged into the *duomo* by devout parents to worship the saint's skeleton.

I never get used to these gruesome traditions. Groups of Catholics line up for Communion to eat "the body of Christ" and drink "the blood of Christ." In the stores, Christ's tears are for sale as the smooth "Lacrime di Cristo" wine, and Judas's blood as powerful "Sangue di Giuda" wine. To me, these names are more poetic than miraculous.

Outside the cathedral, Katy and I nearly get blasted by teenagers with shaving cream. For some reason, people tolerate being covered with shaving cream during the town festival, and even the police laugh when sprayed with foam. An Italian friend, not from Modena, deduced that Saint Geminiano must be the protector of barbers.

Even the housewives are dangerous today. Katy and I ride our bikes near the festival, and an old lady nearly lances me with a twenty-foot-long broom handle for cleaning ceilings that she just bought at the special market for this *festa*. Scared that she wants me to carry her new acquisition back to her house, I dodge her weapon while her friend almost sticks her new broom through my spokes. Every year, the fog festival touts some new miraculous scrubbing device that is finally going to make cleaning fun. This year, brooms with extended handles are the craze. I don't know who has such tall ceilings, but maybe they can clean the entire apartment from their couch.

After we successfully dodge the shaving cream and little old ladies, a man shouts at us over a megaphone to come toward him. He angrily bangs plates on his metal table at his stand but is never able to break them. He yells at us that he has no intention of carrying this set of plates back to Puglia, and if we know what's good for us, we'll buy them immediately. "What are you waiting for?" he yells. "Do I have to come over and rough you up?" Not wanting to get him any more upset, Katy and I pay the thirty euros, which seems like a good price for a bribe not to be beaten up.

We try to hide in the huge crowd to get a look at some

of the other stands. For a while, the fog festival seems like a normal county fair. Kids proudly hold their balloons that look like cell phones as their parents light their cigarettes with cell phone–shaped joke lighters. A Pokémon balloon flies away, and I see Maurizio, the *barista,* trying to console his *bambino.*

The bee man is selling honey to cure every known illness. If he's right, the pharmacies won't be around much longer. The other competition to the drugstores are *erboristerie,* the herbalist shops, selling homeopathic remedies to folks fed up with pharmacies. Today, our favorite herbalist's is full of elderly women complaining about their ailments to the sympathetic young clerk. I don't dare enter.

We go to the candy stand in the market instead. I take a bite into special Sicilian nougat, *torrone,* and nearly break every molar in my mouth. Seeing I'm not satisfied, the woman at the candy stand hands me a rusty pair of pliers and a hammer, insisting that they are actually chocolate. I know that candy stores and dentists work hand in hand, but this is ridiculous.

Guido tells me later this was indeed chocolate, but I wasn't going to risk it. Instead, I seek out a nice juicy hamburger at a food stand, but the other customers in line look at me like I'm a maniac, because eating beef is like playing Russian roulette while mad cow disease runs rampant.

The server at the food stand points to a dead pig head and twists her index finger in her cheek to make the gesture for *buono!* Katy nearly retches. Seeing a crowd drooling over this pig snout wedged up against the glass makes me dutifully wait in line. The delicious aroma wafting out revives Katy, and she helps me devour the *porchetta* wrapped in a piping hot *piadina* flat bread, washed down with fizzy Lambrusco.

The *porchetta* sandwich gives us the strength to line up in the cathedral for an hour to see the holy bones of San Geminiano. A reverent silence falls over the crowd once we enter the crypt to examine the skeleton. The brown bones are free of flesh, and the steadfast jaw of San Geminiano stays shut to show his determination that his bones resist time—surely a miracle. When we leave, somehow the fog doesn't seem so stifling as it gently blankets the city.

Soccer Season

When Italy won the World Cup, fans stripped naked and bathed in the fountains. Train conductors refused to work, and the whole country came to a standstill. Modena suffered thousands of dollars of damage as statues were knocked down and shop windows cracked. It was all great fun, I was told.

With visions of a glorious party running through my head, I accept Roberto's invitation to go to a soccer game. He tells me I haven't lived unless I've experienced the thrill of the stadium when the stands explode in cheers after a goal. I try to hide the fact that the very few goals and endless passes of the ball are mind-numbing to me—all foreplay and no hurrah. Some of the matches even end up tied at zero to zero with no sudden-death shoot-out but are still considered great matches by the fans.

When tournament games are played and broadcast on TV below in Maurizio's bar, announcers repeat in a monotone, "Situazione molto pericolosa" (very dangerous situation). It's obvious when the home team scores because cheers erupt from every house in Vicolo Forni.

I try to be a good sport and agree to meet Roberto at the café across the street from the stadium. The Bar Stadio is jammed with men dressed in their Sunday best, downing shots of espresso and discussing something very urgent.

Roberto is in the thick of the discussion while somehow talking on his cell phone at the same time.

I squeeze into the bar, past these men in their sleek sharkskin suits, Borsalino hats, and spit-shined patent leather loafers. I assume they all are either on their way to or have just returned from church, but when I overhear their arguments and dodge their gesticulating hands, I realize these are actually soccer fans. Perhaps I'm used to American sport fans covering their bellies with logo-ridden sweatshirts, wearing saggy jeans, and waving big "We're No. 1" foam hands. These Italian fans are dressed to kill and are growing more and more agitated with every coffee ingested, and the game has yet to begin.

While continuing both the discussion with his fellow fans and chatting on the cell phone, Roberto greets me across the bar. He taps his watch and points to the door, meaning we're late and have to go. I foolishly ask him if his wife is coming, and he gestures the typical "What are you saying?" hand signal so he doesn't even need to say "Are you crazy?" but he says it anyway.

The line into the arena extends well out into the parking lot, and the more we wait, the more this orderly queue erupts into a mass of people elbowing for position by the door. If the tickets are not sold out, there's no blackout rule that prevents the match from being televised, so stadium goers are the real *tifosi*, or hard-core fans.

Sunday soccer games are never shown live on Italian TV, but most channels feature analysts watching a bank of monitors of all the matches. The usually toupeed TV announcers wipe the sweat from their brows as if the weight of the world were on their shoulders, as bikini beauties wiggle behind them to hold the viewers' attention. "I don't understand why you have *ragazze pon-pon* [cheerleaders] at your football matches. Isn't the game enough?" Roberto asks.

I realize we're in the wrong section for excitement. All the hooligans, or *ultras,* are at the end stands, called *la curva.* Scarves and flags are waved in time to the pounding of deafening drums. Smoke bombs shoot out plumes of the team colors—obviously there's a security leak or a man on the inside allowing these hooligans to sneak their fireworks past the metal detectors.

I went to a couple of soccer games when I was a student living in Brescia, and the *carabinieri* patted down fans for weapons. Another roadblock stopped traffic at the metal detector as some *tifosi* were forced to empty their pockets of coins because industrious delinquents would sharpen them and flick them at the referee. *Carabinieri* in riot gear of flak jackets and thick sweaters circled around the top of the stadium, convinced that the submachine guns they carried would curb violence and peacefully stop *ultras* from running out on the field.

In Brescia, I once sat in *la curva,* at least until an enormous banner was pulled overhead covering the entire grandstand. Some yahoo decided it was a great time to open the last couple smoke bombs and nearly asphyxiate everyone underneath the banner.

The fans are calmer in Modena. At least I thought so until I heard of a Modenese hooligan who was taken to court for being too violent during a game—after all, the Italian word for soccer, *calcio,* means "I kick." The case took more than three years to go to trial, and the verdict passed down imposed the worst possible punishment: the culprit couldn't set foot in the stadium for five years. For a die-hard *tifoso,* this sentence is worse than prison, but on the other hand, how could they actually enforce it? I doubt some bureaucrat calls up the convict every Sunday. Besides, they never check IDs during the elaborate search upon entering the gate.

Once the game finally starts, a hush falls over the stadium. Every head watches as the ball is kicked back and forth and back and forth, almost like a pendulum hypnotizing the masses. No mascots dance around to distract the crowd, and the intercom doesn't blare jock rock. No big scoreboards project instant replays, and the crowd can't be distracted to do the "wave." I'm impressed at how dignified the game and the fans are, until the umpire stops the action. The crowd erupts with deafening whistles, but when the ball is put back into play, quiet follows. The same ball is used throughout the match. If it's accidentally kicked up into the stands, the fans immediately throw it back, not daring to risk the wrath of the entire, impatient stadium.

The first half ends without any score, and I can't help thinking I could have stayed home and watched announcers see the game for me for free. There are no baton-throwing marching bands at halftime, so everyone heads to the bar. Instead of brats and beer, more shots of coffee are in order. Roberto is astounded. "You mean that in America they serve alcohol in the stadium? Don't people fight all the time then? If we had alcohol, we would riot!"

Within seconds of the game resuming, our team plops the ball in the opponents' net on a fluke, since it seems that they aren't quite ready. The stadium erupts in cheers, and complete strangers hug each other, break into song, and then punch quick-dial on their cell phones to spread the good news to those hapless fans who couldn't make it to the game.

In retaliation, the enemy scores a beautiful goal with an elegant butterfly kick, taking our goalie completely by surprise. The *ultras* in the stands at the end of the field start chanting and raising their fists in unison, demanding revenge. The well-dressed men in our section mutter excuses for the home team, and nearly all of them light up a cigarette to calm themselves, sending a cloud of smoke rising from the stands.

The clock ticks away during this high-tension match until just a few minutes remain. Our lead attacker is on a breakaway when a defenseman lands a perfect sliding tackle and kicks the ball out of bounds. The striker falls and grabs his ankle in agony, and the fans break out whistling as though a thousand sirens are wailing. The referee says no penalty was caused and tries to get the game started again.

"It's a scandal! We will never forget this!" Roberto yells.

The hometown coach rushes out on the field and begins shouting at the ref, who ignores him and walks away.

"We know where your car is!" shouts a respectable-looking man at the referee.

Another elderly man yells, "Do you know where your wife is?"

The other men in our section who look like they just came from church start hollering the worst possible blasphemies imaginable in the Italian language: "God is a pig, the Virgin Mary is a cow, and all the saints are dogs!" Perhaps they can seek forgiveness for these digressions next week at confession. Anyway, the priest is probably in the stands too and will understand, considering the circumstances.

The player on the field is still writhing in agony, so doctors run onto the field with first-aid kits and a stretcher. The wounded attacker is gently placed on the litter and carried off the field as the fans clap in appreciation. I tell Roberto this is like American football and the poor player could be paralyzed for life. He looks at me shocked and says in soccer the attacker could be back on the field in minutes. I can't help imagining this elaborate charade is left over from Roman times of gored gladiators being hauled out of the Colosseum.

Immediately afterward, the opposing team takes the lead by blasting another goal in our net almost effortlessly. As the final minutes of the game tick away, the swearing continues to get worse. Christ, Eve, the Host, Judas, and other biblical favorites are paired up with farm animals to damn the referee.

I'm starting to like this game of soccer now that I realize it's about the drama, not the sport. I tell Roberto it was a great game, and he looks at me confused. "We lost! It was terrible." The fans file out of the stadium disgruntled but orderly. Everyone needs to get home in time for the highlights of all the soccer games shown at 8 p.m. every Sunday evening.

The next day, Roberto asks me to put together an article about the game and the difference between American football and Italian soccer. To get his goat, since I'm not a sportswriter, I type that the ball is the wrong shape for football, and besides, for a nation that relies so much on gestures, it's unnatural to only kick and avoid using hands. He laughs and runs the article but titles it: "Our Team Denied Penalty Kick!" At least he puts an appropriate photo of two men arguing.

Modena's soccer team tops its league, so Katy and I decide to go to the biggest game of the season against Reggio Emilia, the neighboring town. Inevitably at the *derby* (when the two local teams play), the fans are notoriously rough. One of my students tells me, "I love soccer, but I can't stand the fans!" I go for exactly the opposite reason. The game is painfully tedious, but watching the fans is where the real action lies.

I ask Guido if he wants me to buy him a ticket, but he thinks we're crazy to go to the stadium for this game. The line for advance tickets—or rather the mob—is dangerous enough with everyone elbowing for a position closer to the box office. People are gathered away from the line; they have sent the best pusher into the crowd to buy a whole group of tickets. When I finally get to the front, I'm mashed against the glass as the woman behind it patiently explains all the different seats. I have to ask people to back up so I can move my face back from the window to pay. Women are charged only a third of the ticket price, probably because they help temper the men's blasphemies.

I bike to Vicolo Forni to pick up Katy after her lessons. Maurizio, the *barista*, is sweeping outside Il Cappuccino, so I show him our tickets. He says he has season tickets so he doesn't have to wait in that horrible line.

Guido tells us to lock our bikes a long way from the stadium, and we instantly understand why. Lines of cops in riot gear surround the stadium, especially *la curva*, so the opposing fans can't get close to each other. All they can do is yell at the opposing fans across the field from the opposite *curva*. Some hooligans try to climb the twenty-foot fences, crawl through the razor wire, and risk being bludgeoned by a *carabiniere* just to punch a Reggio fan. Now that's dedication!

We can't afford the press seats where I sat last time with my editor. From a distance, I see Roberto talking on his cell phone and occasionally covering the receiver so he can yell something at the referee. Our section has slabs of concrete for seats, but no one actually sits. In fact, they're jumping up and down in rhythm as they sing soccer chants. Katy's favorite is to the tune of "Yellow Submarine": "Reggio merda, alé, alé alé!" (Reggio is shit, go, go, go!). It's probably not exactly what the Beatles had in mind. This reminds me that we've seen CDs of soccer chants sung by famous operatic singers. Sometimes, these tenors even have formal concerts just of soccer cheers.

The singing stops and the whistling begins when a Reggio player falls to the ground injured. The Modena fans are especially cruel now. "Vai a giocare con le bambole!" (Go play with your dolls!), they yell.

Modena soundly defeats Reggio, which nearly ensures that our team will move up to a higher league next year. When the buzzer sounds, signaling the end of the match, the Modena players rip off their clothes and strip down to their boxers. The fans go crazy as the players throw their sweaty jerseys over the twenty-foot-tall fences into the crowd. Luckily, we don't get one.

We struggle out of the stadium, avoiding the lines of eager riot cops ready to put their bludgeons to work. Our bikes are only somewhat vandalized with shaving cream, probably by Reggio fans. The fans are still singing in the streets and waving their banners as they walk into the center of the town to celebrate.

Maurizio is back at his bar sipping spumante with his buddies. I ask why he doesn't have a Modena soccer flag up in his bar. He replies, "No real respectable bar has soccer flags inside. It's too controversial, and I'm a professional." Yet when Katy starts singing "Reggio Merda," he can't resist chiming in on the chorus.

Late at night, when we're ready for bed, Katy and I hear an argument in the café downstairs and think Maurizio might be in danger. The shouter steps out on to Vicolo Forni, but we can't understand what he's yelling. Katy says, "Oh, I think it might be a real fight, and I'm worried about Maurizio." The shouts get louder and reverberate on the walls of the alley. We realize even if they are arguing about soccer, it might be dangerous. Just then we hear the screamer walk out to his scooter and say nicely, "Thanks for talking, Maurizio. It was a great game! See you tomorrow."

Truffles and Cotechino

"Yankee go 'ome! Yankee go 'ome!" someone yells into the receiver as Katy holds the phone away from her ear. Rather than worry that this is some sort of terrorist threat against the Americans living in Modena, Katy says nonchalantly, "Here, Eric, it must be another one of your crazy friends," and hands me the phone. A friend of Marina's, Walter, is on the phone, and after repeating his anti-American rant, he breaks into a hearty laugh.

Walter is an ex-journalist who prefers to live in the hills above Modena and raise a variety of breeds of animals rather than suffer the hustle-bustle of city life and deadlines at the newspaper. He proudly participated in Communist rallies in his youth and often breaks into heartfelt hymns to the People in his booming tenor voice. Communism was probably a little too confining for him, and I sense he's more of an anarchist now. Although Walter seems to have come to farming late in life, he's a natural. Almost all of the food he and his wife cook is grown on their land.

Today, though, he's in town to eat at a Chinese restaurant. "I need to get some instructions," he says cryptically. He invites Katy and me to the restaurant for lunch but won't elaborate on these mysterious instructions. He refuses to consider eating lunch at Trattoria Ermes, even though he is old friends with Ermes. "Why should I pay for this kind of food

169

that I can make better at home?" Walter asks. I am mostly curious why Walter needs to go to a Chinese restaurant, because most Italians refuse to eat Chinese food. Italian newspaper headlines consistently warn that missing cats are turned into stir-fry and that outraged Swiss citizens are boycotting Chinese imports after reports of beefy Saint Bernards being served in black bean sauce in Shanghai.

Walter greets us warmly and has already ordered egg rolls and Kung Pao chicken for us. Marina joins us for lunch, too, but doesn't eat. She lives upstairs from the restaurant and has grown tired of the smells wafting into her bedroom.

Not until the end of the meal does Walter reveal his secret. He asks the cook in very simplified Italian, "I have Chinese pig that I want to eat. How do you recommend to cut and to cook Chinese pig?" Walter likes to raise different breeds of pigs to experiment on the best flavor.

"We not eat our pigs!" the cook responds, horrified. "That's disgusting; they're pets! Why would you eat your pet pig?"

After being scolded by the cook, Walter assures me and Katy, "You can eat anything; it's just that some things taste better than others." Even though he doesn't get the proper butchering instructions for his Chinese pig, he invites us to his farm to see the newborn piglets and stay for Sunday lunch.

Katy opts out of a trip to Walter's farm, either because she's wary of eating a pet or else she doesn't want to be at the mercy of someone who revels in yelling "Yankee go 'ome!"

Marina and I drive to Walter's farm in the country. I bring a bottle of some of the best Chianti from the market in Vicolo Forni. I give it proudly to Walter, but he responds, "We have all homemade wine up here, but thanks. We will use this wine for cooking." He pulls out the cork and dumps half the bottle into a sauce cooking in a pan. A big puff of steam fills the air as I stand shocked that such a good bottle is deemed unworthy. Marina explains that Walter doesn't trust corporate winemakers with the pesticides they use on their grapes and the additives they put in the wine. He wants all his food to come from his land.

Walter wants to exchange English classes for prosciutto, a chicken, or wine. I would gladly barter for lessons, but I don't want to take the bus up into the hills and then return with a live chicken or perhaps a small goat to secretly butcher down on Vicolo Forni at night. I'm also a little worried because he wants to learn some good insults, which I'm sure would be aimed back toward me since he likes to be the anti-American revolutionary.

I don't think English is really Walter's language anyway, since his tendencies lean toward the East. He prefers to vacation in Albania. While most people are terrified to set foot in the war-torn Balkans, Walter exclaims, "I would move to Albania in a second! It hasn't been corrupted by corporations."

Lunch is a lengthy but delicious meal of freshly picked *boletus edulis* (porcini mushrooms) stewed with parsley over *tagliatelle*, and, for the more adventurous, pungent truffles. Walter dug these little treasures, and now we shave them over the pasta. I ask where he found these fantastic truffles. "*Attenzione!* You should never ask where someone finds their truffles since it's always a well-kept secret." Marina tells me that fresh truffles are the most expensive food per pound—except for saffron. Walter pokes in the fireplace and from the glowing embers pulls out a *cotechino* (an only slightly less-fatty version of *zampone*) and proudly announces, "This comes thanks to our pigs!"

After lunch, we lounge around in disbelief that we ate so much. Neighbors stop by, and a little old lady grabs me, speaks some indecipherable dialect to me, and makes threatening scissors gestures. She pushes me out the door and sits me down in a chair in a field. She pulls out some shiny scissors and cuts my hair as the other guests laugh. Walter tells me that she used to be the town hairdresser and can't stand to see people with unruly long hair. The neat trim spruces me up, and many people tell her, "Che bel taglio! Sta proprio bene!" (Nice cut! He looks great!).

To help digest the enormous meal, we take a walk. Walter brings a big bottle of homemade *grappa*. We enter the town café, and a group of older men and women at a table suddenly stop playing cards and cover up the money that was laid out on the table. "It's OK. They're with us," says Walter's wife, and the group starts gambling again. They pull out their five, ten, and twenty *lire* coins, which aren't in circulation anymore because they're worth less than a penny.

Espressos are ordered for all, and Walter methodically "corrects" each cup with a swig from his jug of *grappa*. This *caffè corretto* both picks you up and helps you digest at the same time. Most of all, it has a pleasant numbing effect so you just can't feel much of anything anymore.

Back at his house, Walter fills a bottle with his homemade *grappa* for me to take back to town. I ask him jokingly if it will make me go blind, but he answers matter-of-factly, "No, this one won't because of the special valve I've recently installed." Somehow, this doesn't calm my fears.

His wife, Maria, then fills a plastic container with some of the fresh porcini sauce for us to take home. Walter is worried. "If you don't bring me back my Tupperware, I will kill you," he warns. "I've always wanted to kill a Yankee, so you could make my dream come true." Since Walter contentedly cooks his pet pig, I give him back his Tupperware so he doesn't get any ideas about cooked Yankee.

Porn and Puritans

"Mamma mia! I'd like to have the job of painting those posters!" says my visiting friend Dan when he sees the porno posters around town with all the dirty parts covered with gray paint.

The porn cinema is located next to a touristy pizzeria, across the street from a playground, and in the same building as a church. Looking in from the street, I can see the lobby has a big brass statue of a naked couple in some difficult position with arms flailing in the air in ecstasy.

The newest porn poster for a film features two "actors," a Bill Clinton look-alike standing majestically in front of the White House with a far slimmer Monica Lewinsky–type woman on her knees grasping him around the waist. The idea of an ex-president in a porno flick isn't exactly attractive, but the poster is such a beautiful parody that I must have it—and there's not even any need for gray paint on it.

Guido, Katy, and I go inside and beg the older woman behind the counter to give us a copy of the poster titled "Sex Gate . . . Scandal of the United States." She looks at us suspiciously but finally sneaks us a couple of copies of the poster, realizing we aren't the police. Outside the theater, we open the poster to admire our acquisition. A group of Italians on their evening stroll notice it and say, "Bill Clinton was the most powerful man in the world. He could have any woman he wants, so what was he doing with that intern? She's not even pretty!"

In Italy there's a different sense of humor about sex, which perhaps explains its love affair with Cicciolina. The Hungarian-born porn star campaigned through towns topless to draw crowds and eventually she got elected to parliament. When Saddam Hussein invaded Kuwait, Cicciolina took a sensible position to the impasse. She offered to sleep with Saddam Hussein if he'd pull out of Kuwait. Saddam, like a fool, ignored her, and look what happened to his country.

Having grown up in the relatively puritanical United States, I'm generally shocked by these displays. I suppose we Americans are hypocritical, though. The whole Clinton-Lewinsky affair disturbed so many people, while many of the Republican and Democrat accusers and political vultures had similar little liaisons behind closed doors.

An editorial in my hometown newspaper in Minneapolis laments salacious new magazine advertisements by declaring, "New ads are like soft core porn." Italian newsstands, on the other hand, relish in advertisement posters featuring full nudity for the cover of *Gente* (Italy's *People*) and all the most popular magazines. Only the real hard-core magazines are lucky enough to get a swath of gray paint over women doing panty pulls.

Italian friends are quick to point out Italy is only second in porn consumption after the United States. Or as one of the distributors at the Sexpo convention noted to a journalist, Germans like extreme sadomasochistic porn, Americans like slick, glossy porn, and Italians like funny, amusing porn.

In Italy, sex isn't as shameful as in America. What else could explain the appearance of porn diva Moana Pozzi in Italian commercials for furniture, cars, and chicken patties?

Ms. Pozzi, star of *Moana: Deep Hole,* appeared regularly on prime-time talk shows discussing literature and films with director Federico Fellini. They also discussed, of course, her craft. "Obscenity is sublime," she said. "Pornography is the representation of our most intimate dreams, our most secret desires." When she died in 1994, Italy fell into mourning. A conservative Catholic journalist wrote after her death that she was a good little girl who "left the gate open." People beseeched the Pope to canonize her as "St. Moana the Virgin" or perhaps "Holy Moana of the Sacred Taboo," according to the *New Yorker.*

The Holy See didn't agree that this sinner should be sainted but nevertheless sponsored the Jubilee in the year 2000 to forgive the sins of the believers. They also allowed believers to pass through La Porta Santa, a Vatican doorway opened once every twenty-five years to wash away their sins. This Catholic ability to forgive lusty transgressions would surely have benefited Clinton, and perhaps even he could become a hero of sexy Italian TV ads.

La Tivù

Living in the center of town surrounded by brick buildings, we have terrible reception for the TV (or "la *tivù*," as it's called here). Down at the bar, Maurizio gets perfect reception. He explains he has an electrician friend who tapped into the big antenna on the roof and ran a line down the outside of the building. The work had to be done on a Sunday, so the *carabinieri* police wouldn't notice.

Changing the outside of the building in any way is illegal because the historic center of town is considered a museum. Once we hung out some clothes on the window ledge to dry—just as we'd seen on postcards of alleys in Italy. Within the hour, two neighbors warned us it's illegal, and we should take them in or risk a *multa*, or fine, from the police. Putting a few bottles out on the ledge to chill puts neighbors in a tizzy. They asked if we were trying to kill someone, because the bottles could fall onto Vicolo Forni. Strange how no one is upset now that we have put out flower boxes.

We ask Maurizio if we can rig up our TV to his antenna, but he says it's much too risky. This is probably another ploy to get us to come down to his bar more often. Then he adds, "If you come down to Il Cappuccino, then you don't have to pay the television tax."

Television tax? A few days later, we receive a letter in

our mailbox from the RAI national television station stating we are required to pay sixty dollars or risk having our TV confiscated. We don't even get good reception!

We call up Guido to ask what we should do. He says, "I never pay it. In Naples, nobody pays, but everyone here in Modena pays it like a bunch of sheep. I wouldn't worry about it. If they do come by to check, just make sure you cover the TV and try not to let them in the door. If you are caught, you only have to pay for the past two or three years."

This seems typical of dealing with Italian bureaucracy. Avoid complying with the law until you're caught. For example, the Italian parliament wanted to prevent endangered species being killed, so it passed a law requiring everyone who owns exotic fur coats or any other product made with these animals to register at the *questura* within a few weeks. (Most of the older women I teach have at least one, and sometimes up to ten, minks.) People panicked, and endless lines formed at the already overcrowded police stations. The day before the deadline, outraged politicians forced the parliament to nullify this law because it unfairly hassles citizens. Millions of Italians wasted hours of time, and the fur owners who just sat on their hands laughed.

We take Guido's advice and ignore the tax on our TV. Instead, we invest our money in a brand-new *RADAR* antenna, so we can at least have reception. Soon, we're watching ads, which are the best way to learn the language and arguably the most interesting aspect of Italian television. A phone company ad of cell phones playing soccer appears, and Katy shouts, "That's Italy! That sums up everything about Italy! Well, almost. Maybe the winning cell phone should get a pizza."

Just then the door buzzer rings. We ask at the intercom

who it is, and a man with a very low voice replies that he's from the RAI. Katy frantically covers the TV as I nervously open the door. Guido pops his head in and laughs. How gullible we are! He invites us out for a pizza to celebrate all the money he's saved from not paying his TV tax for eight years.

Politics, Italian Style

I t's election season again. Anyone who can get hold of a bullhorn is marching up and down the Via Emilia first thing in the morning stumping for their party. Enormous posters of smiling politicians munching on cigars are tacked up wherever there's wall space—even over all the porno movie posters with the swaths of gray paint covering the dirty parts.

The old men in the piazza are especially worked up. Betting on fierce card games of *scopa* usually creates a silent hush for the card counters, but different factions have formed along party lines, with the occasional infiltrator sneaking into another group to cause an uproar.

The sidewalks are clogged with tables piled high with postcards, stickers, and petitions. A fed-up citizen stops me to sign a demand to end corruption in the government; she needs only another fifty signatures. When I explain I'm not Italian, she tells me, "That will look all the more impressive! Besides, you don't believe anyone actually checks all these signatures, do you?" I suppose not, so I sign it.

The mailboxes are jammed every morning with different party brochures, and the postman's bicycle overflows, leaving a trail of colorful flyers in his wake. Political pamphlets are shamelessly—but perhaps truthfully—called *propaganda* in Italian. Last year's model is out of fashion, so this

179

year's batch promotes all sorts of old parties with new names for the ever-fashion-conscious Italians. Few people want to be associated with the once powerful Socialists since the former Socialist prime minister, Craxi, avoided being jailed by fleeing to Tunisia, where he passed away. The Christian Democratic leader, Andreotti, who led the fight against organized crime, has been indicted on charges of colluding with the Mafia. Out with the old corruption!

Communism has never looked so good. Unfortunately, just when the tide was turning to the left, the Communist Party quarreled and broke into about four subparties. To win in the upcoming elections, the losing left wing has consolidated its many factions to appear strong, in spite of vast differences in views. Once elected, the coalition can sort out their problems and hopefully avoid dissolving yet another government.

The major competition to the left wing is led by the richest man in Italy, Silvio Berlusconi, an ex–lounge singer who owns a soccer team and a few television networks, which broadcast his message 24/7. He's known for gaffes, such as the time he said that "Mussolini never killed anyone. Mussolini sent people on holiday to confine them," and more recently "complimented" Barack Obama, saying, "He's young, handsome, and even tanned." Under the moniker Forza Italia! (after a soccer cheer meaning "Go Italy!"), he managed to unite a right-wing coalition of the ex-Fascists with the notorious Northern League. The "reformed" Fascists have strong nationalist tendencies, while the Northern League wants the rich north to secede from the rest of Italy and realize their dream of becoming an independent country called "Padania."

Berlusconi already served as the country's prime minister a few years ago when this same coalition of bizarre bedfellows fell apart over obvious differences. He then dodged millions of dollars in tax-evasion fines and corruption charges—a feat that endeared him to Italians, who marveled at how he worked his way around the country's monolithic bureaucracy. "He, more than anyone, knows where the corruption is and how to fix it," one of my students tells me. "Let's just hope he's rich enough so he doesn't need to accept any more bribes!"

Campaign tactics are devilishly clever. But this year, protest candidate and porn diva Cicciolina isn't wowing the crowds by parading through town topless. Perhaps her campaign isn't so compelling anymore since all her porno posters have been covered up with political posters.

Guido points out a sudden spurt of road construction blocking many streets is an attempt by the ruling party to show the electorate that it's actually doing something. These work projects are often abandoned after the election, depending on the winner. If the right wins, then the left-leaning unions stage constant strikes. If the left wins, the big business leaders refuse to pay taxes.

One of my students is fed up with the tax system. She asks if I'm renting *in nero* ("in black," or under the table), and I realize my landlord never did give us a lease, so perhaps we are renting illegally. She assures me the apartment owners aren't paying taxes if we don't have a contract. Somehow knowing that I'm skirting the law opens her up to reveal her tax situation. She owns some apartments but rents them illegally because the taxes are 50 percent on them. This is why she's voting for Berlusconi; he would lower taxes. Then she could be honest and start paying her share. I'm a bit skeptical that potential taxpayers would start popping out of the woodwork to come clean.

In any case, the wide array of political parties in Italy

covers the spectrum and will satisfy any palate. Anarchist parties try to organize occasional rallies but have a hard time keeping it all together. Monarchists fly the old Italian flag with the crown smack dab in the middle of the green, white, and red *bandiera.* They still resent Mussolini for ousting King Vittorio Emmanuele III—perhaps one of the few worthwhile things Il Duce did. Still, trading monarchy for Fascism was hardly a step in the right direction.

My friend Marina is sick of the whole situation so has decided to run in the city elections. The local Green party has agreed to take her on as a candidate, even though she's a journalist for the newspaper *L'Unità,* founded by the most famous and respected Italian Communist, Antonio Gramsci.

Almost all of my friends from Emilia-Romagna are quick to pronounce themselves Communists. While most of the rest of the world has ousted Marxist leaders, Italy has embraced Communism, with "Red Bologna" as its capital—odd considering this is one of the wealthiest cities in the country. Many Bolognesi resent it when others are richer than they are. Perhaps Communism is the great equalizer that will make everyone well off. At least they throw a great party every year, La Festa dell'Unità, which lasts for weeks, offering bands from around the world and cuisine from across Italy.

Other friends admire the U.S. system, with its "stable" two-party system instead of the confused and sometimes corrupt world of Italian politics. On election day, however, only about a third of Americans cast ballots, while nearly every Italian votes, even though they often have to go to where their official residence is. If they don't vote in three elections in a row, their right to vote is taken away, and they have to fight a mountain of bureaucracy to get it back.

The morning after the elections, the bum on Vicolo Forni

is loudly announcing the winner to anyone who will listen. Some people stop to listen to his diatribe and usually end up arguing with his position. In an attempt to sway the opposition, the bum offers his listeners a swig from his bottle of sweet red wine.

The elections are over. Italy has its fifty-eighth government in fifty-five years. A new prime minister still has to be elected by the senators, if the tenuous coalitions hold. Marina seems relieved she didn't win but is nevertheless upset some of her friends didn't vote for her. They say a vote for her would have been just a protest. Obviously her campaign couldn't match Cicciolina's topless brigade.

The old men in the piazza seem to be friends again. While gathered over a scooter seat, they have drawn new battle lines over heated card games. The posters will stay glued to the walls until they're covered up by next year's political *propaganda*—or more pornography. Meanwhile, schoolkids with bright-colored backpacks draw mustaches, profanity, and genitalia on the hapless politicians' faces.

I uncover the TV—confident that the RAI tax man isn't watching—and switch on the *telegiornale* evening news. Berlusconi has been inaugurated as prime minister. Rather than using his position to earn more money, he's using his power to avoid corruption charges. In protest, left-wing politicians walk out of parliament blindfolded.

A few days later, the *telegiornale* features two senators waging a fistfight as their colleagues try to hold them back. Worried a revolution could take place during the transition of power, I call up Guido for the whole story. He gives me the scoop. One of the senators told the other that his soccer team was going to lose in the big match tonight. Politics were set aside in favor of a battle over soccer. In other words, life is back to normal.

The Art of Eating

"Please don't be offended if I ask you something," one of my students said shyly. "I've heard that in America sometimes the people—not you, of course—take the food home that you don't eat in restaurant. You call it 'doggy bag,' but these American people—other people, not you—don't give this food to dog but eat this old food. Is it true?"

When I tell him it's very common, he's awestruck, "You Americans—I mean they Americans—are animals!" When I explain that sometimes Americans eat sitting on the couch watching TV rather than at the dining room table, he exclaims, "No, no. This I cannot believe."

I'm constantly corrected about my eating habits. We were given a beautifully designed bowl that we use for sugar. When we show an Italian friend, he exclaims, "Sugar bowl? No, this is a cheese bowl! What if someone puts sugar on their pasta? Their whole meal would be ruined. I think it's best you put cheese in here." The explanation that grated Parmesan looks vastly different from crystal sugar doesn't hold water. We are forced to replace the sugar with cheese or face questioning and warnings whenever guests come over.

"What is the typical dish of America?" one of my students asks. While I list many things, the other students rebut that these are European foods. "Hamburgers are from Hamburg in Germany. French fries are French, or Belgian." They think I'm holding back information when I tell them we eat food from all over the world.

In Italy by contrast, it's difficult to find food other than the specialty of the area, and visitors expect they can get ravioli, chicken Parmesan, spumoni, and other supposed Italian staples wherever they go. When an American couple visits, they want to relax after a rough trip driving down from Milan. "Once we get a nice bowl of spaghetti, things will be fine," Warren exclaims. He's not happy to hear it's almost impossible to find that on the menu in Modena. "What? They don't even serve spaghetti here? We're in Italy, aren't we?"

Despite many Italians' love of food, I rarely see anyone who is fat (Pavarotti being the exception that makes the rule). The only overweight woman I met in Modena moved to North Africa because, as a friend told me who has been there, "Gli piacciono i ciccioti" (they like 'em chubby). She has become a successful lounge karaoke singer at an African resort.

My students constantly barrage me with the question *Perché gli americani sono così grassi*? (Why are Americans so fat?). Perhaps a better question is why Italians aren't fat even though they spend so much time at the table.

When I'm invited to people's houses, they consider themselves good hosts if I eat everything in sight, but then they worry that they didn't have enough food for me to eat. It's a battle. If I don't eat enough, they're disappointed; if I do eat enough (according to their standards), I'm so painfully full I feel sick and never want to eat again. I've discovered my culinary heaven, but I'm required to indulge in so much of this angelic food that I pray for a respite.

This is why I'm worried when my parents come to visit. When Ermes learns my mother is in town, he insists I bring her to his *trattoria* so he can feed her. After much fuss she finally does go for lunch, but Ermes doesn't really have anything to say to her. Instead, he sits her in the place of honor. *La mamma* is to be respected, after all. My mom says she feels as though she's been put on display, like she's a cardinal holding court. "Buon giorno, signora. Buon giorno. Piacere," the other diners politely say to her as they pass in front of her.

A class of friendly students invites my family over for dinner to help make risotto with *frutti di mare* (seafood). The hostess, Valentina, has been to the United States and bought an American flag with a bald eagle on the top of the flagpole. "Bellissimo," she says as she pulls it out of the closet and removes the protective plastic. It had never been out of the closet since she brought it home. Perhaps as a lighthearted mockery of the American patriotism they see on TV—or maybe to make my parents feel at home—these adult students parade around the living room carrying the Stars and Stripes and humming the tune of our national anthem. My dad, who never misses a chance to break into song, belts out the words to "The Star-Spangled Banner." We all join in to perpetuate the stereotype.

The parade of dinners continues as another class wants my parents to come to one of their houses, with the rest of the class along to make sure everyone eats enough. At his house in the flat Po Valley, the host grabs my father by the arm to show him the cellar where all his homemade sausages are strung up from the rafters. This is a man's job to examine the hefty supply of pork for the year. When they return from the larder, my dad tells the host how impressed he is, and I can't tell if he's serious or just a champion bullshitter. My dad tells me, "He said that we're the only Americans he's ever seen."

The student interrupts, "No, no! You are the only *skinny* Americans I've ever seen!"

While my dad is respected and allowed to inspect the pork supplies, my mother is considered a celebrity. At this dinner, the host proudly brings out a tiny bottle of his special forty-year-old balsamic vinegar for my mother to examine. My mom pops open the top of the bottle, and the classmates cringe. The host just wanted to show the bottle to impress her, not to have her meddle with it. He bites his lips when she pours a hearty spoonful and swallows it. However, she is *la mamma* and can't do wrong, so they courteously ask her if she likes it.

"Delicious! I've never tasted anything like it!" she says, and her faux pas is forgiven.

Eating Venus's Navel

"If you manage to make tortellini, when you return home to America, you'll have lots of friends!" says *la nonna*, the grandmother of one of Katy's students.

We've gathered for a day of making fresh pasta at *la nonna's* little house. After she shows us the Moto Guzzi that belonged to her late husband, we're ready to get to work. Or rather, Katy and *la nonna* are ready to roll out the pasta, but I'm not allowed too close to the kitchen table because I'd get in the way.

Instead, I'm in charge of writing down all the recipes as *la nonna* recites them to me, half in dialect, half in Italian. Many of the quantities are "just a dash," "as much as you need," and even "a little bit," making duplication of her recipes at home nearly impossible. "There's no secret; once you make the pasta, you learn," *la nonna* advises, but we've already tried making fresh pasta at home and ended up hungry with flour all over the floor and a ball of glue. Obviously, we need the guiding hand of an expert.

La nonna describes how she learned to make pasta from her grandmother, and she from hers, and so on. *La nonna's* daughter doesn't have time to learn how to make pasta, so the tradition in her family may be lost. She's happy we're interested. She says, "I've taken Katy on as my student only because I know that she's serious and really wants to learn. You know, in the old days in Modena, if a woman didn't know how to make pasta, nobody wanted her!"

The aprons are tied, the eggs and flour are mixed, and the pasta is rolled. Like a painter with her brush, *la nonna* handles her four-foot-long rolling pin while teaching her new apprentice. Soon the yellow pasta is so thin it fills the entire table and hangs down off the edge almost to the floor.

They begin with *tagliatelle, cestini* (little baskets), *farfalle* (butterflies), *maltagliati* (badly cut ones), and *quadrettini* (little squares). To make the grooves on *maccheroni, la nonna* wraps a little square of pasta around a stick and rolls it on the strings of an old loom. When I ask who thought of doing that, *la nonna* responds, "No one knows! We only know it was simply a stroke of genius!"

Now for the most difficult filled pasta: tortellini. In the past, I have made the mistake of wanting all sorts of different fillings for pasta—seafood, mushrooms, artichokes—but most Modenesi consider me a perverted American. Tortellini can only have meat filling, usually with prosciutto, *mortadella* (bologna), and ground pork. If they don't have meat inside, they simply aren't tortellini. Period.

Luckily, *la nonna* isn't so rigid. When I ask about other fillings, she says what's fun about cooking is experimentation. But first the basics. Drop a bit of meat on a small square of pasta, fold the dough over the dollop, and wrap it around your pinky. The shape of tortellini is scandalously based on Venus's belly button. The tortellini are supposed to be small enough to fit ten of them in your palm.

La nonna finally lets me try, but I don't have her knack. She comforts me with an old proverb, "Don't worry, because 'pane e tortelli quando son cotti son tutti belli.'" (Bread and tortelli when they're cooked, they're all beautiful).

Tortelloni, on the other hand, are bigger and slightly easier, and tradition isn't so strict with the filling. Spinach and ricotta are standard; pumpkin and nutmeg are permitted. Meat, however, is out of the question.

The last pasta *la nonna* shows Katy how to make is ravioli. "Ravioli aren't from here, they're imported, but we'll make them anyway," says *la nonna*. In Italy, if a specific dish comes from the next town over, it's considered foreign food.

After eight hours of rolling fresh pasta, Katy's arms are exhausted, but *la nonna* is still going strong. We stop for a break of *gnocco fritto,* essentially fried dough, with some prosciutto and Parmigiano-Reggiano. While we're eating, *la nonna* pulls out a pasta maker and tells Katy proudly, "In 1973, they gave me this machine, which is now a relic, but I've never used it! These machines change the flavor of the pasta so it comes out tough. I'm going to give it to you, but I advise you never to use it!" Katy accepts graciously but is confused why she is receiving this gift she must never use. *La nonna* continues, "To get good at pasta, you have to make it at least once a week. We make it every Sunday. In America, if you don't find work, you could open a tortellini store!"

Following our pasta-making experience, Roberto publishes my article in the weekly about Katy's pasta lessons from *la nonna*. Now, everyone on Vicolo Forni asks Katy how her pasta making is coming along and if she's going to open a shop. The older men compliment me for having her learn to make fresh pasta, because so many of these young Italian women are essentially a lost generation. Franco's wife gives her advice on the best tools for making pasta. The woman at the photocopy shop gives Katy her not so secret recipe for tortellini and tells her butcher to expect an *americana* who will be ordering her special mix of meat. Friends and neighbors fish for an invitation to taste the tortellini, but Katy can't keep up with all the demand. Instead, she's undertaken an equally revered Italian pastime, *sciopero* (strike).

Back to High School

"You want me to teach high school kids?" I ask the principal of a local Modena high school. "They'll eat me alive!"

He assures me they are very well behaved and respectful, but I remember attending a year of Italian high school in Brescia and my out-of control classmates. The students stay in the same classroom all day, so the teachers must enter enemy territory. I tell him I have to mull it over.

My Italian friends Guido and Sonia say I must accept immediately. They tell me that many friends have studied for months to take a huge exam with nearly a million other Italians to get a job as a teacher. Only a couple hundred positions in schools will be open, making their chances a statistical improbability. The school offered me the job without any sort of qualifications, simply because I'm a native speaker.

I meet with the principal again and explain that I'm technically not allowed to teach in Italy since I don't have a work visa. He looks concerned and tells me, "We are a public institution, and everything needs to be as clear as the light of day, so I will ask the school accountant if you can work here." The principal informs me later in the day that the accountant ("he's very good") found a loophole in the law that allows me to work part-time. On the one hand, I'll be working for the government schools; on the other hand,

191

the government can throw me out of the country because I'm illegal. Another Italian irony.

When I arrive for my first day of classes, an ambulance is parked in front of the school, and a student is being hauled out on a stretcher. No one seems too concerned, however. I ask if she's OK, and one of the janitors tells me, "She just passed out; it happens all the time."

Classes are half English lesson and half wrestling match. Once I finally calm the students down, they are very good at expressing themselves—like Fulvio, who reads a poem in halting Shakespearean English about medieval sword fights to the confused class.

When I finally do understand what they're talking about, I try to correct their choice of words. They, in turn, correct me by showing the British word in their textbooks: time-piece, trainers, braces, jumper, and so on. We read about a British entrepreneur who likes to smoke and "is obsessed with fags."

The first lesson, I ask them what important monuments I should see as a tourist in Italy. Although this seems like a fairly serious topic, they manage to find a way to turn it into a ridiculous lesson. One insists the Leaning Tower of Pisa is in Florence, much to the amusement of his classmates. They don't put even the Colosseum in Rome, the *duomo* in Milan, or St. Peter's in Vatican City on the list. The soccer stadium in Milan is near the top of the list. This sparks arguments about the best players, and some of them pull their team scarves out of their backpacks to wave around.

The principal interrupts one of the classes of older students, who are preparing to go on their *gita scolastica,* or school trip, to Paris for an entire week. The *gita scolastica* is a time-honored tradition in Italy. At the end of nearly every year, each high school class ventures to another city or site for a day or two of fun and alleged education. The principal explains, "The insurance didn't work out for your trip, so you have to promise to be on your best behavior." The students put their right hands over their hearts, raise their left hands, and say, "Giuro, we swear we'll be good." I'm amazed the principal accepts this and lets this wild group invade France.

When they return, I ask if they visited the many museums and monuments on their itinerary, but they spent most of their time at the Moulin Rouge and then slept during the day. I feel sorry for the poor teacher who had to accompany them. I ask if they at least ate some great Parisian cuisine. "Ugh! Fa schifo! French food is awful. We ate spaghetti every night, and even that was barely edible!" I have Italian friends who go to exotic places and always search out Italian restaurants. Inevitably, the Italian food isn't as good as in Italy, so they're always disappointed.

I convince my high school students I don't speak any Italian, so they have to speak English. Even when they say something in Italian and I translate into English, they still don't realize I can understand them.

My scheme backfires, however, when I'm teaching a lesson about the vocabulary on driving. They carefully write down steering wheel, shifter, accelerator, and horn. "'Orn? You want to say *clacson*, no?" For some reason, Italian uses the antiquated English word *klaxon* for horn. To explain without speaking Italian, I fake I'm honking a horn and say, "You know. Beep! Beep!" The whole class looks at me in disbelief. I do the gesture again and say, "C'mon! Beep! Beep!" Then I realize I'm doing the vulgar Italian gesture for screwing, complete with sound effects.

At that point, the lesson never recovers. Luckily, the bell

rings, and the tackling begins. The battle to get out the door is only the precursor to who can get on their scooter most quickly to zoom away. One of my students points out the window to show me his tiny new 50cc car. What parent in their right mind would let a thirteen-year-old go forty miles per hour in a little tin can in vicious Italian traffic?

James, a twenty-year-old British teacher, instructs high school students as well, and when students misbehave, he makes them do fifty push-ups. Personally, I tend to avoid corporal punishment because the students seem to punch each other enough when they joke around.

I tell my students to just call me "Eric" (pronounced "Ay-deek" by Italians), but their strong sense of formality holds them back. Instead, they usually refer to me as *prof* or sometimes even *dottore* since a regular bachelor's degree from an American university makes me a doctor in Italy.

I keep teaching evening classes in the school for adults as well. I'm surprised at how the old habits learned in high school die hard. I ask one of the adults if she's done her homework. "I didn't do it, to be in solidarity with my ill classmate Gabriella," she tells me seriously. When Gabriella, recovered from her cold, attends the next lesson, she solemnly thanks the woman for her solidarity. At first I thought this was just a ruse to escape homework, but their heartfelt camaraderie was more important to them than possibly upsetting the teacher, me.

James teaches another evening class and decides to have a lesson of English profanity. I have a soft spot for profanity as well, but I've found whenever I give swearing lessons, it comes back to haunt me. In fact, the following week, two female students ask me, "The other English teacher, James, use much word 'shagging' with us. What it mean? He like very much say 'shagging.'"

Before I can respond, an Italian teacher explains matter-of-factly, "It's a British slang word that means to take someone from behind."

"Oh," respond the two disgusted students.

Then I jump in, "Actually it's more like *'fare l'amore,'* to make love."

Suddenly they break into big smiles and exclaim, "Oh! Then it's a beautiful word, and we will use it often!"

Somehow, James's list of English profanities is left on the chalkboard after the evening class, so the next day the high school students busily copy it down. Soon, all the students are far more interested in learning English.

La Ferrari

It's Sunday morning, and the sound of mosquitoes flying everywhere wakes me up at 5 a.m. The scary little plug-in insecticide device won't get rid of the bugs this time. Then I realize the buzzing emanates from Maurizio's bar below us, where the regulars are watching the Formula One race, live from Malaysia. I consider asking him to turn down the TV, but then I hear the noise coming from nearly every one of my neighbors' windows.

Modena is the land of automobiles: Maserati, Lamborghini, De Tomaso, Bugatti, Stanguellini, Cizeta, but most of all Ferrari. Enzo Ferrari built his first factory in town and then moved it nearby to Maranello. Modena claims Ferrari as its own, and every Formula One race calls for an unofficial holiday because what else could possibly be more important?

The Ferrari logo is pasted everywhere. Even a computer mouse in the tourist office is colored Ferrari red and has race car driver Michael Schumacher's signature imprinted on it. While in the United States every classroom has the Stars and Stripes hanging in the corner, Modena's have Ferrari posters.

The high school students I teach ask if I root for Ferrari, and I have little choice but to say "yes." This puts me in their good graces; otherwise, why would they pay attention to a traitor? To prove my supposed interest, I tell them about a video I saw of a Ferrari driving full speed at dawn from one end of Paris to the other in twenty minutes with pedestrians diving out of the way. For once, my students are speechless in amazement. One of them lifts his jaw and exclaims, "*Bellissimo!* Very beautiful! This my dream!" Italian law is very wise to forbid teenagers to get their driver's license until eighteen years of age.

My students ask how powerful my car's engine is back home, and I feel like a fool when I have no idea. "At least you know the maximum speed of your automobile, no?" I explain that U.S. speed limits don't allow us to reach the car's top speed. They don't quite understand, and soon the class breaks into chaos as some students insist Italy has speed limits too. The naysayers point out, "No one is ever ticketed, so essentially there is no law, right?"

The word *safe* doesn't really exist in Italian. *Sicuro* is just "secure." My students suggest *non pericoloso* (not dangerous) but add that everything has a certain amount of danger, so "safe" is a paradox.

Later, one of my adult students who works at the Ferrari factory asks me to clarify American product liability laws that just allowed Porsche to be sued for making a car that accelerates too fast. "How is that possible? *Troppo veloce?* How can a car be too fast?" As the futurist F. T. Marinetti wrote, "speed is beauty," so how can something be too beautiful?

Ferrari's Formula One zooms from zero to one hundred miles per hour and back to zero in seconds. I ask one of my students if these cars are dangerous. He works for one of the many high-tech cottage industries that construct parts for Ferrari's race cars. He scoffs. "Soccer is responsible for many more injuries," he assures me. "In these last twenty years of

Formula One, only five people have died, and they've usually been spectators."

Katy suddenly shows an interest in going to San Marino to see the next Grand Prix, but I tell her I'd get the same satisfaction lying by the side of the *autostrada* watching traffic. One student promises us that seeing a Formula One race would be very memorable because the cars are the loudest thing he's ever heard. "It's very beautiful, but bring earplugs or you won't be able to hear for a couple of days." With this encouragement, I agree to go to San Marino with Katy only if she can sit through an entire race on TV beforehand.

The weekend of a Formula One race arrives, and Japanese and German Ferrari fans appear in Modena's piazza decked out head to foot in bright red Ferrari garb, in stark contrast to the somber, stylishly dark clothes of Italians.

I ask my students who work at the Maserati factory what time the race is, and surprisingly most of them don't know. One student shames his colleagues, "If you worked at Ferrari, you'd be fired!" I don't dare remind them that Maserati is actually managed by Ferrari.

Before the race, I hear from my old roommate that Signor Truffino, the boss of the Lord Arnold School, was watching an interview with Ferrari's race car driver Michael Schumacher the other day. The journalist scolded the German driver for not understanding Italian and then turned to the camera, asking, "Isn't there anyone out there who can teach this man our language?" As if the interviewer was speaking directly to him, the boss yelled to his TV, "It's me! I can teach him Italian!" He called up the Ferrari factory in Maranello and offered free lessons for Schumacher, but none of his teachers would do it for the measly pay that Truffino offered. "It's an honor!" he explained to persuade the un-convinced teachers to do it for almost nothing.

Maurizio at the bar downstairs tells me that at the same time as the race, Piazza Grande will be full of classic old cars built in Modena. He's working on getting a Ferrari in Vicolo Forni in front of his coffee shop to draw in customers.

The little old lady who lives upstairs tells us, "Oh, I'm definitely going to watch the race. I'm a big fan!"

Carlo at the candy shop is a little more skeptical. "Every-one is for Ferrari, so I've decided to be different. I'm for McLaren."

Maurizio doesn't believe him. "How can anyone support McLaren and come from Modena? It's impossible! Carlo is only saying that to get in arguments."

The day of the race, slick Maserati spiders, antique Stan-guellini race cars, and, of course, spectacular red and yellow Ferraris fill Piazza Grande. The little old lady upstairs is out walking her dogs and tells us, "The cars are beautiful, so, so, beautiful!" Although she has a hard time walking, she wants to drive one as fast as possible.

Maurizio wasn't able to fit a full-sized Ferrari into Vicolo Forni, so a large toy Testa Rossa on a stand will have to do. Parents plunk twenty-five euro cents into the machine, and toddlers can fulfill their dream of driving a race car and be jostled around in the little fiberglass Ferrari with real rev-ving noises. When the *bambini* get too agitated, *la mamma* pulls them off so they don't lose their lunch.

At race time, the streets are deserted. Everyone goes home to watch the televised race from Monte Carlo. Il Cap-puccino, however, is crammed, and everyone is giving a running commentary. An occasional pop of a Lambrusco cork can be heard as Maurizio fills glasses. Katy tries to watch the race on TV but lasts only a couple of laps. Now my hearing will be spared from having to see a race live, and a few hours of buzzing mosquitoes every weekend isn't too bad.

The ghost town fills up when the race is over. Following any Formula One competition, it's better to lie low at home. The fans are often so inspired by the race that they hop in their Fiats and reenact the race on the *autostrada*.

Road rage is rare in Italy. Perhaps Schumacher's stoic German personality is a good influence because it doesn't allow for emotion; he only wants to win. My student who works on Formula One parts for Ferrari tells me, "This is why women shouldn't drive. It's terrible. They're very dangerous. Very, very dangerous." He shakes his head sadly as if millions have died because of these ridiculously permissive laws allowing both sexes to share the road. Then he confides he bought a car with a small engine because he always drives as fast as the car will go and then gets in trouble. He confesses, somewhat ashamed, "My new car only goes 180 kilometers per hour." I calculate his car exceeds 110 miles per hour, and I'm sure he buries the speedometer needle.

In a recent survey, Italian drivers were rated the third worst in the world, following South Africa and Turkey. I'll say in their defense, Italian drivers are absolutely fearless, which, I suppose, could also be called courageous. They know the exact width of their car and are not afraid to barely miss any obstacle (including pedestrians) by millimeters. Unfortunately, horrible auto accidents are regularly splashed across the front page of newspapers. Journalists sometimes criticize the dead drivers not because they weren't cautious or went fast, but because they couldn't control the car better.

I explain to my students that we in the United States practically live in our cars. We often eat or drink beverages while driving. Some people even shave or put on makeup behind the wheel. Inevitably, my students are shocked, and one responds, "We don't eat while driving because it would make our cars dirty."

Word spreads about how bad American drivers can be because another U.S. teacher who has been in Italy many years can't get an Italian license without taking years of supplemental driver's training. "They gladly recognize licenses from Uganda and Mozambique but won't recognize my U.S. license after three years of driving here!" she complains. I don't dare tell her that Italians probably respect African drivers because they can drive through crazier cities than Naples. Perhaps Italians view the African drivers as worthy competition on the road.

That's why it's the dream of every Modenese—and Italian for that matter—to own a Ferrari and floor it on the *autostrada*. One of my students, Antonella Ferrari, granddaughter of Enzo Ferrari, can have as many sports cars as she wants. Ironically, she doesn't like driving them. She always arrives at class on her bicycle with her bodyguard, who waits on Vicolo Forni during the lesson on his little one-speed. When I ask if she owns a Ferrari, she tells me, "Oh yes, but when I go in my Ferrari, the people look at me and want to race. I prefer the bicycle in Modena." Many bicycles, however, proudly sport Ferrari's black stallion. This way, even a pleasant bike ride turns into a race.

The day after the big Formula One race, my student who works at Ferrari agrees to give me a tour of the factory in Maranello. This town, just outside of Modena, lives and dies for Ferrari. Every Grand Prix race is projected on an enormous screen in the piazza for everyone to see. Two years before, when Schumacher nicked his rival's car and was flung from the track, an elderly man had a heart attack and died in the piazza. These are serious fans.

Before touring the Ferrari factory, I stop at a gas station to find out who won the race, so as not to look like an idiot. The attendant eyes me suspiciously. He doesn't bother telling me who won, but only that Ferrari placed third. When I say *Molte grazie* a little too cheerfully, he scowls at me.

The factory seems a surprisingly nice place to work. The sound of water dribbling over a little fountain in the corner isn't exactly the Trevi fountain, but it keeps employees' minds from wandering to the beaches of Rimini. Displays of classic Ferrari motors around the factory remind workers of the reputation they must uphold. No big robots clang infernal noises at breathtaking speed; rather the cars are ratcheted together by real live humans with cigarettes dangling from their mouths in spite of "Vietato Fumare" signs. Somehow they manage to catch the dangling ash and not sully the spotless floors or the perfectly buffed cylinder heads. To get around within the factory, workers ride little bikes plastered with Ferrari stickers. As in all Italy, the espresso machine is the most popular spot in the factory, at least until lunchtime.

Only in Italy could the lust for beauty and perfection produce these fantastic handmade cars. Only fifteen cars a day are finished and displayed at the end of the assembly line.

My student points to one of the cars and says it has an expanded driver's seat for the American market. "We found the biggest eater in the company cafeteria, put him in a prototype, and let him take a few laps." My student points out, "He's a very big man and very important to our quality control."

The back part of the factory is strictly off-limits. "The Formula One area is top secret. It's our Area 51," he says, as if they're working on some UFO special project. He recommends I see the Ferrari test racetrack on the way back to Modena but skip the Cavallino restaurant because it's just for tourists, who steal the forks and plates with Ferrari logos.

After the tour of the factory, I return to teach the wild kids at the high school. During English lessons the day after Ferrari wins, time is inevitably dedicated to discussion of the race and the fantastic maneuvers of Schumacher. If Ferrari loses, it's better I don't even mention it. Today, however, the topic revolves around my factory tour.

"Do you see the gallery of wind?" one asks in stilted English. I reply that the wind tunnel, designed by Renzo Piano, was off-limits. "Oh, is a sin! Is most important monument in Italia!" Another student interrupts, "No, no! Cicciolina the porn star is the most important monument in Italy!"

All of the students, even the girls, have visited the Ferrari test track in Fiorano. I tell them about a couple of people who had the chance to ride in one of the Formula One cars on the track and vomited profusely afterward. They dismiss this and say, "Yes, but it's very beautiful!"

After its last victory, twenty-one years ago, Ferrari has finally won the world championship.

The little old lady upstairs is walking her dogs on Vicolo Forni and nearly cries with joy. She tells us it's the happiest day of her life. Maurizio puts out an enormous banner in Vicolo Forni with the Cavallino black horse, which fills the entire street. When the wind picks up, the flag nearly knocks people off their bicycles. No one dares say anything, probably out of fear of being seen as anti-Ferrari.

My student who works at Ferrari assures me this victory is far more important than the Italian soccer team winning the World Cup. After all the body, engine, and frame are all made in Italy. I argue that at least the Italian national soccer team has all Italian players but Ferrari has a German driver, Michael Schumacher. "But he drives for an *Italian* team: Ferrari," he explains. I don't understand, but it makes perfect sense to most Italians.

That evening, I walk by the city hall, and a closed-circuit TV is broadcasting to a small crowd in the piazza. Michael Schumacher is being declared an honorary citizen of Modena and given the keys of the city. After a lengthy speech by the mayor, Schumacher manages to say in a strange Italo-German dialect, "I'm happy to be here in Modena." The audience is thrilled he can finally speak their language, even though the mayor then asks him a question, which he doesn't understand.

After this year, Ferrari wins easily—too easily—and the fans are never satisfied. Maurizio at the bar complains, "Schumacher is like a robot; he never makes any mistakes. It's boring!"

As though to placate Maurizio, Ferrari doesn't place first in the next few races, and his bar fills up once again at five in the morning for the final race of the year. Even Carlo from the candy shop stops us before a race and whispers, "Cross your fingers for Ferrari!"

Touch Your Balls for Luck!

A recent survey reported just under half of Italians believe in the evil eye. My students assure me those people are just gullible and scared. When I tell my Italian high school students that we Americans are terrified of the number thirteen—no thirteenth floor of skyscrapers, no room number thirteen in hotels, no row thirteen on planes—they think we're crazy. "Doesn't the person in the fourteenth row realize it's the thirteenth?" they ask me.

While they taunt me about the world's only superpower being superstitious, horoscopes feature prominently in Italian magazines, and Italians are constantly "touching metal" with their index finger and pinkie to ward off the evil eye. I explain it's the equivalent of knocking on wood, but they laugh at how simple we Americans are.

Apart from the usual four-leafed clovers, never opening an umbrella inside, and throwing the pieces of a broken mirror into a stream, many more superstitions are followed—or, more appropriately, obeyed—in Italy. When walking with Italian friends on the street, I notice little idiosyncrasies but soon realize many people have a whole series of habits to bring good luck and avoid the bad. With all these possible pitfalls, it's a wonder anyone even steps out of doors.

If you don't wear a scarf when it's the least bit chilly, a cold isn't the only disease that will strike. Even the healthiest will surely fall victim to the dreaded *colpo della strega* (the witch's hit) and should thank their lucky stars if they survive.

Watch where you walk. Some towns have an *arco del cornuto* (the cuckold arch) that if you pass under, your lover will betray you. When I walk under it, my friends' jaws drop, and they ask, "Even if you don't believe it, why do you risk it?"

To undo the damage done, try to squeeze between a couple *carabinieri*. These special policemen always walk in twos, reportedly one to read and one to write since they're notoriously dim. Woe be to you if you walk between two nuns, however, since the holy power of the church will certainly damn you! Otherwise, find a lit cigarette butt someone has thrown on the ground and stamp it out to take all the luck of the smoker. If you miss the cigarette and hit dog doo, the mitigating factor to consider while you're cleaning your shoe is that this is the absolute best sign of good luck.

The Italian national pastime of sitting around the table for hours is fraught with peril. If you're unmarried, never sit at the corner unless you plan to stay single for the rest of your life. When clinking glasses, never cross arms with fellow toasters across the table, unless you feel like playing Russian roulette. Making a cross means some poor soul in your midst is doomed. If you sit down at the table and your utensils are crossed, the host is obviously damning you. Only the foolhardy sit thirteen people around a table; the number will be reduced to twelve either voluntarily or forcibly by unseen powers.

Pouring wine calls for proper etiquette as well. Never pour overhand with your wrist turned outward, or the recipients will be insulted. Also, make sure their glasses are filled before your own; however, you can sneak the last drop for yourself to ensure all the romantic interest from guests with the opposite hair color will be aimed toward you.

While spilling salt is bad news, accidentally tipping over your wine glass is good luck. To make sure this good fortune sticks, dab your finger in the wine and put a little behind your ear. A friend's mom makes the rounds with the spilled wine and blesses everyone with a little drop on their necks.

Being careful at the table is the only way to avoid leading a damned life in Italy. Perhaps that's why they never vary from their schedule of eating lunch at 1 p.m. and dinner at 8 p.m. Never. When I ask my students about this, one of them pipes up, "I eat a bistecca [steak] every day!" without fail. Then the mad cow scare hit, so I'm sure she's reassessing her dangerous ritual now.

Students are the most superstitious. Apart from having special pens, charms, and lucky clothes, my high school students refuse to hop over a chain that blocks courtyards to keep out scooters. Bottlenecks form as students try to squeeze around these chains, and the janitors, who set up the whole situation, just laugh. Luckily *professori* usually understand why the class is a few minutes late, since we once were students ourselves.

I catch some carrying a little *peperoncino* (red hot chili pepper) or a small horn to ward off evil. They tell me it's just for fun and characteristic of southern Italy. It's a little more difficult for them to hide making the *corna* gesture. They stick out their index and little finger (like the American rock 'n' roll gesture) and vigorously point their fingers downward to avoid being jinxed.

I explain in America we cross our fingers to prevent bad luck. The boys stand up and say, "In Italy, we touch our balls!" They dig their hands into their pockets, unashamed. "Touch your balls, professore; it's good luck!"

I pass on the opportunity to be an exhibitionist teacher. I

should just change the subject, but I can't help asking, "What do girls do?"

The boys stand up again, grab their privates, and yell, "Girls must touch my balls! Touch my balls!" Luckily the principal isn't walking by the classroom. That's another thing; just mentioning the name of the principal is bad luck and leads to failing a test.

The lesson has already digressed, so I ask my students to list all their superstitions. Each myth requires comments, however. Never wear purple on TV ("It's true! No one ever dares risk it!"); if a bat pees on your head, your hair won't grow ("It's a myth, but I do always wear a hat at night!"); if you're sweeping and you brush your shoes, you'll never marry ("I insist my mamma always does the cleaning."). They even have a twist on the old umbrella doctrine: "Opening an umbrella inside only gives bad luck to the eldest person in the room!" This leads a few of the students to threaten to open their umbrellas to curse me. Surprisingly, they don't do it, since this is really no joking matter and they worry about being expelled.

Now that they've explained their system of beliefs, I know why all the boys seem to be digging into their pockets with a look of fear every time they hear an ambulance or see an empty hearse go by. They don't want to be next.

While I write about these superstitions, I realize I've become more careful myself while living in Italy. I don't pass under ladders, I never toss my hat onto the bed, and I can't possibly kill a spider (much less a seven-legged one). On the dreaded day in Italy, Friday the seventeenth, I don't plan anything too important.

Why Would You Ever Leave?

It's spring, and the fog has lifted from Modena. Even the bum is sporting slick new sunglasses. These shades make him look more like the Unabomber than someone to pity enough to give alms. Eventually, he shaves his face—perhaps to get a better tan—and puts on shorts for summertime.

Vicolo Forni is finally closed off to traffic, and daisies fill new flower boxes lining the busy alley. The old lady upstairs lets her little dogs loose. They are thrilled at these new flowery targets to pee on. Cars still try to squeeze illegally through the tiny street, causing curses from passersby forced to back up against the wall to avoid the jutting mirrors.

The bum seizes the opportunity of the new traffic congestion. "Avanti!" he yells to oncoming traffic and carefully leads the Fiats through the mass of pedestrians. The next day, he puts on a fake sheriff's badge and comes armed with a whistle for added authority. No one hesitates to dutifully obey his orders; perhaps they're relieved, since the real traffic cops are never around. Finally, the bum has found his calling, and he'll do it for free—as long as he can sip his wine on the side. Some drivers even tip him, so in a sense he's our new police force.

Now some residents of Vicolo Forni want to get rid of the public telephone around the corner. An older woman warns me, "The only ones who use that phone are the brutta gente [ugly, or bad people]." I assume hers is another excuse to get rid of the *extra-communitari* (people from outside the European Union). Then one day, I hear a guy yelling into the phone in English, convinced no one can understand him, "I got your drugs! Come and get them!"

The bum is a sort of watchdog against these illegal operations. One day, though, as he complains to us about the *extra-communitari*, I point out that Katy and I are foreigners too. He says, "You know that's not what I mean . . . "

In any case, we know that we'll have to go back to our home in America eventually. In the meantime, we find we have a bike we don't need anymore. We want to give it to the bum, but Maurizio, the *barista*, tells us the real police came and asked him to leave. "He'll be back next week," Maurizio assures us. Later in the day, we see the bum wearing a new parka and a Modena soccer hat, and riding around a bicycle far better than our squeaky old wreck. Obviously, he'll be fine, even if he has lost his begging job on Vicolo Forni.

After two years of living in Modena with Katy, another school year is almost over, and all our Italian friends are planning their six-week vacation to the mountains or seaside—even the weekly newspaper is taking a summer break. After weighing the pros and cons, Katy and I decide to move home and perhaps return to Italy in a few years. We'll move out of our apartment and give up our Italian life to be closer to our relatives and maybe start our own family. Italian friends are shocked when we tell them we're leaving. "What do you mean? Do you really hate Italy so much? You have a job, a beautiful apartment, good food. What more could you want? Minnesota must be better, no?"

The idea that we came to live in Italy for a short time is completely foreign to most all of them. All but two of my classmates from high school still live in Brescia. Living any-where besides one's hometown is like exile and surely tem-porary. Guido moved north from Naples. Although he likes Modena, he constantly pines for the south. Recently, a cor-rupt government official left the country to escape being thrown in jail. After five years he returned because he missed real Italian pizza.

One of the schools owned by my crazy old boss, Signor Truffino, is moving from Vicolo Forni as well. After the heated arguments, the threatening letters, and being labeled a "risky subject" by the boss, nothing could have prepared me for what happens next. One of the school secretaries calls me up to say the school is moving to a location out of the center, but she has a problem. A French class still wants to meet in Vicolo Forni, so the secretary asks if I'd be will-ing to host a French class in my apartment. I'm shocked. On the one hand, the school wants me to do them a big favor; on the other, the boss tried to sue me over a "virtual con-tract," withheld my paycheck, and threatened to get me deported. Does the school realize how absurd the situation is? Fortunately, the French class finds a real classroom in-stead of our cozy little kitchen.

When we break the news of our departure, the *mammas* of the kids who Katy teaches are furious. "Who will teach my bambino next year? Of course you have a replacement to send us, right?" Katy is speechless when the mothers don't even say they'll miss her or at least *grazie*. One of the *mam-mas* says, "Oh Katy, why do you refuse to learn Italian?"

Fed up with the doting *mammas,* Katy jokes, "I'm not leaving until I have these Italians bowing to me!" Later that day, as we're walking out the door to Vicolo Forni, my old boss is moving out boxes from his school. Just as he's bend-ing down to adjust the doormat, Katy steps on the mat. She hovers over the bent-down Signor Truffino, who doesn't even notice her. Katy looks at me and says, "That'll do."

My last day at the high school, I lead all my students in a sing-along to a song my band back home recorded called "Bake My Pie." They pay attention and listen intently while writing the lyrics in their notebooks. New vocabulary is written on the board: "crust," "filling," "preheat," and so on. One student asks what "pie pan" means, so I mime the outline of a pie tin with my hands. It's a trick, and they all burst into guffaws. Apparently, I did the well-known gesture for *Ti faccio un culo così!* which means "Your butt is going to be this big when I'm done sodomizing you."

Just at that moment, sirens wail. I'm saved by an earthquake drill. Another English teacher pops her head in and yells that the students need to march single file outside and put their arms on the shoulders of the student in front of them. This is a sure recipe for headlocks and punches, but somehow they make it to the parking lot. The teacher must fill out complicated bureaucratic forms while the students run around amid the parked Fiats and Vespas. "How many students are missing, and how many were hurt in the evacuation?" she asks, as though injuries are standard during these drills.

The teacher complains about being so full after her big breakfast this morning. "I thought of your American breakfasts when I had coffee *and* milk." I keep expecting her to add "eggs, bacon, pancakes, French toast, etc.," but I now know that Italians consider milk to be a meal in itself.

Back in the classroom, I tell my students I'm leaving for the United States soon, and I hope they've learned a lot of English. I realize that's wishful thinking when they say, "Salute me, Britney Spears. She is very bee-aaa-ooo-tiful girl!"

They want to treat me to an espresso at the school bar. I know my lessons didn't teach them much when a student asks me, "Come si dice 'bar' in inglese?" (How do you say *bar* in English?). When I tell him it's the same word, he replies, "Oh, you use the Italian word *bar*!"

I bid my students *addio*. I stop in the principal's office for my paycheck, which I assume is ready. When I initially signed the contract, I told the administration that American schools pay every other week, and they were shocked. Here in Italy, I was supposed to get half the pay midway through the semester, but it didn't come. They then assured me the entire sum would come at the end. Now, the secretary tells me the whole sum will come a month after I leave the country. "Trust us," she tells me. I use the "breaking their balls" technique I learned from my Milanese friend Anna. I explain they've already breached the contract, and I am wary. Short of going to the *questura* and filing a *denuncia*, I'm left with little choice but to trust them.

I try the *brutta figura* technique, telling the principal I have to pay the final installment of rent on the apartment. I don't want to make a fool of myself because the school wouldn't pay me, but I can call the landlords and tell them that his school is cheating me out of my paycheck. This he understands, so I assume he'll pay me immediately. Instead, he offers to call up the landlord to give his personal assurance she will be paid. Miraculously, the money comes through.

I stop at the newspaper to say good-bye to my editor, Roberto, but he's busy working on his new state-of-the-art laptop computer. I ask what happened to his last computer, and he responds, "They stole my laptop." I'm not sure who "they" are, but I imagine the other people in the office who were tired of listening to him blasting Nirvana's "Smells Like

Teen Spirit." Now, Roberto slips in a DVD of *Blade Runner* and turns it up full blast. "The speakers are much better on this computer anyway!" he yells.

I tell him I'm leaving, and he is so upset that he calls me a traitor for abandoning him and Italy. When I tell him I want to attend an Italian master's program at an American university, he softens his stance and asks if he can come too. "Oh how wonderful on the American campus with all those ragazze pon-pon [cheerleaders] fawning all over you!" Roberto actually believes movies like *Animal House* show "real" college life.

I ask if he would write a *raccomandazione* (recommendation) for my application to the university. He's offended and says, "Eric, I'm not like that. We don't do that kind of thing here!" Apparently *raccomandazione* has Mafia connotations, as in vouching for someone who's on the take and proposing an offer they can't refuse.

He insists on *salutarmi bene,* which I translate as "saying good-bye to me well." In other words, we have to go out for a pizza. That evening at the pizzeria with his wife and Katy, Roberto sets his new computer on the tablecloth and puts in a DVD. "It's just like at home. We can watch TV and eat pizza at the same time!" Finally, his wife convinces him to shut off the computer, but then his cell phone rings. Duty calls. There's another breaking story about soccer hooligans.

My friend Antonio is not surprised we're leaving. "I'm amazed that you made it this long here with all these conformists!" He then invites me to appear on his television show to talk about my time in Italy. Every week, Antonio appears on local satellite television and somehow finagled NATO to sponsor him to air his ideas to the world.

Being on Italian TV sounds glamorous, but to reach the

studio in an old run-down farmhouse, we have to dodge a ferocious dog. Antonio warns me the dog is nothing compared to the enormous pungent man in the tech room, who often delays his program arguing about whether the old Donald Duck comic strips are better than the new ones. "He knows everything about Disney, UFOs [pronounced oo-fos], and dinosaurs in movies," Antonio tells me, sounding impressed.

Today, though, we're sidetracked because the technician is outraged by the faulty special effects of the film *Independence Day*. "If a space station blew up, it wouldn't have a ring-shaped explosion, but the fireball would extend out spherically. This is space; there's no gravity!"

We finally get into the studio after another half-hour debate about plausibility in sci-fi movies. Once we're on the air, Antonio asks me my impression of neighboring Bologna. I respond that it's a beautiful city and I can even imagine living there someday. Right after I utter these words, I realize I've been set up.

The next day back on Vicolo Forni, the butcher teases me, "So you like Bologna better than Modena, huh?" This momentary lapse of loyalty to my host town was broadcast throughout televisions across the region. I've fallen for this trick before, and now I'll never live it down.

On Vicolo Forni, Ermes is parking his bicycle to go into the market for the daily shopping. I'm worried he, too, will come after me for admitting I like Bologna too. Maybe he'll put his death grip around my neck again, but he starts chatting with Katy instead. The old woman from upstairs sees them and says, "For shame, Ermes; she's far too young for you!"

Maurizio, the *barista*, steps out of Il Cappuccino and pulls me aside. I'm worried that I'm going to be scolded for not honoring Modena enough on television last night. No, he wants to personally show me the new "DO NOT ENTER" road sign that replaces the old *senso unico* (one-way) sign. I don't want to burst Maurizio's bubble by pointing out that even though traffic is prohibited on Vicolo Forni, cars even now struggle to get through from both directions.

Later in the day, I see Maurizio defy the new sign as well. He pulls up into the alley in his station wagon. He unloads some tables and umbrellas for outdoor seating. I'm excited. For our last couple of days in Italy we will enjoy a nice sidewalk café with music, maybe accordions, playing in the evening. Instead, Maurizio runs a clandestine antenna line from the roof to hook up a big TV in the alley. Franco, the pet-store owner, and the other regulars now spend all day watching the Grand Prix race, rooting for Ferrari under our window.

They crank up the volume another ten decibels because of all the honking horns. I assume a line of cars is trying to illegally sneak through the alley but then notice the banners waving. Modena's soccer team won another game, so now they will move up into the B league next year. The police are busy putting boards over the fountains to prevent revelers from taking public baths, as they did after the World Cup. Maurizio pops open a bottle of Prosecco to celebrate. Franco turns to me and says, "This is indeed a great day!"

I'd like to stick around and watch the Grand Prix in Vicolo Forni with them, but we have to pack to leave tomorrow morning. When I enter our apartment upstairs, Katy is hanging up the phone. She tells me it was a solicitor offering to come to our place to give a free presentation on mozzarella cheese.

"Of course you said 'yes,' right?" I ask, thinking we could get regular delivery of fresh mozzarella to our door every week.

I'm shocked she declined. "We can go downstairs for cheese in the market. Besides, we're leaving tomorrow!"

I know she's right, but I start contemplating the cost of importing a water buffalo to Minnesota to produce extra-fresh mozzarella every day. Just then, Guido calls to invite us out for pizza. He tells us the mozzarella salesman routine is a well-known scam in Italy. "They know people's weaknesses," he warns. Guido saves the day by giving us a *buon viaggio* gift of fresh mozzarella his *mamma* just sent up from Napoli. "You must eat it immediately for it to taste the best," he advises. "And do not put it in the refrigerator!"

We go to bed early because we have to depart at 4:30 tomorrow morning to catch our train. Guido has agreed to bring us to the station, but he doesn't realize we have six suitcases and a boxed bicycle. In his little red Fiat, he illegally enters Vicolo Forni—there are never police in the early morning. Miraculously, we fit everything inside or on top of his tiny car.

We envision a long, teary *addio,* with hugs and stories about our time in Modena. We'll reminisce about the best meals of super *zampone* or the perfect pizza in Naples. We can chat for hours about the finer points of prosciutto and mozzarella. I'm worried that Katy and I will convince ourselves to stay and eat the fantastic food of Modena for the rest of our lives.

Then the train barrels into the station—on time, like Mussolini promised. We fling open the door and hurl our bags on the train. The train only stops for four minutes before the conductor blows his whistle to shut the doors. We manage a hasty *arrivederci* to Guido through the windows as the train carries us away from our life in Modena.

Parli Italiano?

acetaio	place where vinegar is made
addio	farewell
amore	love
Ape	three-wheeled Vespa made by Piaggio; literally, "bee"
apertivo	aperitif, before-dinner drink
argomento	subject
arrangiarsi, arrangiati	figure out or work the system to your advantage
Ascolta!	Listen! (used at the beginning of nearly every conversation)
autostrada	highway
Avanti!	Go ahead!
Babbo Natale	Father Christmas
bambino	baby, or child
bandiera	flag
barista	barkeep; plural, *baristi*
bel paese	nickname for Italy; literally, "beautiful country"
(fare) bella figura	to cut a good figure
bimbo, bimbi	babies, kids
bis	encore, again
biscotto, biscotti	cookies

Borsalino	a brand of hats made from beaver felt, the perfect topping for any self-respecting mafioso
brava, bravo	good, clever, good job!
briscola	trump; also, an Italian card game
(fare) brutta figura	to make a fool of yourself (the opposite of *bella figura*)
Buon giorno!	Good day!
buono	good
bustarella	bribe
calcio	soccer; literally, "I kick"
calzone	literally "trouser leg," but usually folded stuffed pizza
Camorra	Neapolitan Mafia
campanilismo	pride in your town; literally, loyalty to your *campanile,* or church tower
cantuccini	almond biscotti, a specialty of Siena usually dipped in sweet Vin Santo
Capito?	Understood?
cappuccino	coffee with foamy milk in the shape of a *cappuccio,* or hood, like Capuchin monks wear
carabinieri	one of the police forces in Italy (and also the butt of countless jokes)
casino	chaos, craziness; literally, "whorehouse"
casinò	casino (with stress on the last syllable)
cavaliere	knight
cervello	brain
Che bellezza!	How beautiful!
Che schifo!	How disgusting!
ciccioli	extra pork parts mashed together with extra fat and eaten as an appetizer

clacson	car horn (from the English word *klaxon*, deriving from a U.S. patent)
conservante	food preservative
cornetto	croissant; also called brioche, un *pasto*
denuncia	denouncement, indictment
la dolce vita	the sweet life
Il Duce	title given to Benito Mussolini
due	two (pronounced "doo-way")
duomo	cathedral
erboristeria	herbalist shop
fare l'amore	to make love
frutti di mare	seafood; literally, "fruit of the sea"
furbo	sly
furbone	shyster, wise guy
gabinetto	bathroom
gelataria	ice-cream shop
giovanotti	youths
gita scolastica	school trip
Giuro!	I swear it!
gnocco	dough that is usually fried or baked. Not to be confused with *gnocca*, which refers to a beautiful woman or her privates. Usually singular, since *gnocchi* are dumplings.
grappa	Italian firewater distilled from leftover grape rinds after making wine
grazie	thanks
imbroglione	swindler, cheater
impiegato della posta	postal employee
interrogazione orale	oral exams
la vita è dura	life is hard

ladri	thieves
Lambrettista	Lambretta scooter rider
Lambrusco	fizzy red wine from Emilia. In the United States, this is the headache wine that teenagers love; in other parts of the world it is considered "red champagne."
lepre	hare
lira, lire	Italian currency that has been replaced by the euro
liscio	Italian polka; literally, "smooth"
lite	quarrel
maiale	pig
Mamma mia!	literally, "My mother!"
mammone	mamma's boy
Mangia!	Eat!
merda	shit
micio	kitty
minestra	soup, usually with just broth and pasta
miracolo	miracle
Modenese, Modenesi	from Modena, or a person from there
modulo	document, form
molte grazie	many thanks
mortadella	Bologna's bologna
motorino	moped
muratori	construction workers, carpenters
nero	black, or "under the table"
non c'è male	not bad, no problem; literally, "there isn't bad"
la nonna	the grandmother
orecchi	ears

orecchiette	ear-shaped pasta from Puglia
palazzo	apartment building or palace
pandoro	sweet, yellow Christmas bread; literally, "bread of gold"
panino	sandwich; literally, "little bread"
Parmigiano-Reggiano	Parmesan cheese
passeggiata	a stroll
pavone	peacock
pavoneggiarsi	strut like a peacock, show off
pepperoncini	hot red peppers, usually dried and used mostly in southern Italian cooking
permesso di lavoro	work permit or visa
permesso di soggiorno	permission to stay, temporary visa
piacere	pleasure, or "pleased to meet you"
piazza	town square
piselli	peas or penis
pizzaiolo	pizza maker, usually from Naples
polenta	cornmeal mush
polpetta	meatball
porcellino	little pig
porcini	*boletus edulis* mushrooms, usually wild
preservativo	condom
primo piatto	first course; literally, "first plate"
propaganda	information, originally from the Vatican office "de propaganda fidei," the propagation of faith
prosciutto crudo	raw ham
puttana	whore

puttanesca	literally, "of the whore," but the name of a hot pasta topping. I heard three explanations for the etymology of this spicy sauce's name: 1. It uses ingredients that a woman who isn't a happy homemaker would have handy, as they keep a long time in the larder: capers, anchovies, garlic, olives, pepperoncini. 2. A whore uses these strong flavors to cover up the smell of all the other men. 3. This sauce makes you horny for a whore.
questura	police station
ragazze pon-pon	cheerleaders; literally, "pom-pom girls"
ragazzi	guys, boys
ricatto	blackmail
risotto	a rice dish cooked with a variety of ingredients and a base of broth and onions
salumificio	salami factory
schifo	disgusting; usually *Fa schifo!* (It's disgusting!)
sciopero	strike, often *fare sciopero* (go on strike)
scontrino	a receipt
scopa	an Italian card game; literally means "sweep," but in slang also means "screw"
soggetto rischioso	risky subject
tabacchi	tobacconist
al taglio	by the piece
tazza, tazze	cup or toilet
telefonino	portable cell phone

terra	earth
terroni	derogatory term for southern Italians
Terronia	derogatory term used by northern Italians for southern Italy
testa quadrata	square head (what Modenesi call people from Reggio Emilia)
tifosi	sport fans
tigelle	little biscuits from the hills of Modena usually eaten with lard, Parmigiano, and sometimes prosciutto, *stracchino* cheese, and arugula
tivù	TV
tortellini	meat-stuffed pasta shaped in the form of Venus's navel
trattoria	informal restaurant
tristezza	unhappiness. *Che tristezza!* means "What sadness!"
troppo veloce	too fast
uao	wow
uccello	bird, or slang for penis
uomo	man
uovo	egg
va bene	OK
vaffanculo	fuck off; literally, "go do a butt"
Vespa	scooter made by Piaggio; literally, "wasp"
Vespisti	Vespa riders
Vietato Fumare	No Smoking
vino	wine
zampone	boned pig trotter; literally, "big shank"

Acknowledgments

Auro e Alberto the crazy musicians; Sonia Arcaro for showing us the south; Sebastiano and Rosaria Ascione for *gli spaghetti alle vongole*; Bruno Baccari and his Moto Parillas; Guido (e la mamma) Breccia for the advice and mozzarella; Fiorella Buonagurelli; Barbara Calenzo; Cristina Cocchi; Anna Cornia; all the Cremoninis; Nives Dotti; Anna Erba for teaching me how to break their balls; Giovanni Erba and his theories of everything; Julie Fast from Boring, Oregon; Antonella Ferrari; Marco and Roberta Fontana and their cat 'fanculo; Letizia Franciosi; Francesco Garello at Maserati; Sonia Gentilomi for offering me the job and understanding when I had to leave for love; Franco and Giordana Gregorini for keeping watch over Vicolo Forni; Lynne Rossetto Kasper and the balsamic vinegar conference; Elena Keeper; Garrison Keillor; Mary Keirstead; Pasquale Lambiase; Valentina Luciani for marching with the American flag; Stefano Marchetti; Paolo Marucci at Ferrari; Antonio Mascello for publishing the Italian edition; Giulia Muti; Mike Nilles for opening the door; Anna Pagnoni; Serafino Panissidi; Carlo Pedrazzi; Maurizio Pulega for the best *cremino* in Modena at Il Cappuccino; Liliana Romeo and Massimo for renting us the most beautiful apartment in Modena; Mathilde Rosano and Salvatore; Silvano Rubino; Valeria Ruggeri; Francesca e Bona Scianti; Giovanna "la nonna" Tagliazucchi for taking care of us; Walter "Yankee Go 'ome" Telleri; Tobias and Wilma; and Davide Tognetti for his Italo-American slang.

Friends and family back home have put up with my Italo obsession and inability to stop gesturing: Carol and Paul Berg, who treated us to fancy food; Jay Dregni; Nickle S. Hook; Bob and Cheryl McCarthy; Jim and Judy Mundt; Todd Orjala; John "Italia" Perkins; Meredith Sommers; Margaret Tehven; Dan Tomassetti and his dad for the feasts at Trattoria Ermes.

Great editors waded through numerous revisions both in Italian and English: Hans Eisenbeis, Julie Caniglia, and Tom Bartel at *The Rake* (R.I.P.); Chris Welsch and Kerri Westenberg at the *Star Tribune*; John Lurie, Don Ross, Julie Schumacher, Patricia Hampl, and Mimi Sprengnether at the Creative Writing Program at the University of Minnesota; Kathy Rider, Ornella Lavecchia, and Susanna Ferlito at the Italian department of the University of Minnesota; Ronald Martinez at Brown University; and mostly Roberto Serio, Cecilia Lazzeretti, and Marina Leonardi in Modena, who published the original versions in Italian.

The Minnesota State Arts Board believed enough in this project to donate some funds, and Torskeklubben gave me a generous two-year fellowship and kept me fed on cod and giant boiled potatoes while I finished this manuscript and *In Cod We Trust*.

I thank the Italian Cultural Center and Concordia Language Villages for helping with this project, as well as all the fantastic staff and villagers at Lago del Bosco who kept my interest in Italy alive during all these years.

Eric Dregni is assistant professor of English at Concordia University in St. Paul, Minnesota, and dean of the Italian Concordia Language Village, Lago del Bosco. He is the author of several books, including *In Cod We Trust: Living the Norwegian Dream*, *Minnesota Marvels: Roadside Attractions in the Land of Lakes*, and *Midwest Marvels: Roadside Attractions across Iowa, Minnesota, the Dakotas, and Wisconsin*, all published by the University of Minnesota Press.